DECLUTTER

The Japanese Art of Minimalism

By Phillip Lark

Copyright © 2018 A.C. Drexel
All rights reserved.
ISBN-13: 978-1986267823
ISBN-10: 1986267822

© **Copyright 2018 - All rights reserved.**

The contents of this book may not be reproduced, duplicated, or transmitted without direct written permission from the author.

Under no circumstances will any legal responsibility or blame be held against the publisher for any reparation, damages, or monetary loss due to the information herein, either directly or indirectly.

Legal Notice:

You cannot amend, distribute, sell, use, quote, or paraphrase any part of the content within this book without the consent of the author.

Disclaimer Notice:

Please note the information contained within this document is for educational and entertainment purposes only. No warranties of any kind are expressed or implied. Readers acknowledge that the author is not engaging in the rendering of legal, financial, medical, or professional advice. Please consult a licensed professional before attempting any techniques outlined in this book.

By reading this document, the reader agrees that under no circumstances is the author responsible for any losses, direct or indirect, that are incurred as a result of the use of information contained within this document, including, but not limited to, errors, omissions, or inaccuracies.

Table of Contents

Introduction 1

Section I Minimalism: The Starting Point 5

Chapter 1 - The Minimalist Mindset 7

Chapter 2 - Benefits of Minimalism 28

Chapter 3 - The Transition 35

Chapter 4 - What Matters the Most to You? 44

Section II Declutter: The Art of Tidying Up 53

Chapter 5 - A Life without Clutter is a Happy Life 55

Chapter 6 - A Tidy Home 73

Chapter 7 - A Sprint, Not a Marathon 78

Chapter 8 - Less Is More 83

Chapter 9 - Breaking the Habit of *'Just in Case'* 90

Chapter 10 - Categories Are Key 100

Chapter 11 - Use of Space 104

Chapter 12 - New Beginnings Are the Best 113

Conclusion 125

INTRODUCTION

Minimalism and decluttering go hand in hand. Marie Kondo was the first author who showed the world the art of Japanese minimalism. Since her popular book about decluttering the home and owning less, the movement to adopt certain mindsets and philosophies around minimalism has grown.

Japanese minimalism is based on the traditions of Zen Buddhism. Buddhism is the primary religion or way of life in Japan, with Zen being a school of the original Buddhism as created by the Buddha, Siddhartha Gautama. Buddhists believe that you do not need material objects to be happy and reach a state of Nirvana.

There are degrees of minimalism, such as becoming as minimalist as possible. Sasaki Fuimo is an example of such a person who decided to change his lifestyle. It was not a matter of money but a conscious choice to believe less can be more. Fuimo let go of his collection of CDs, books, and DVDs. He decided it was not essential to follow the trends that said you should own material things to be like everyone else. Fuimo, like many who opt to adopt the Japanese art of minimalism, used to always think about what was missing in his collections and what he needed to buy next when, finally, he came up with the answer.

It was not what he lacked in possessions and trendy items that was the problem, but it was all about time. He spent too much time cleaning and shopping, instead of spending time with friends, traveling, or going out and enjoying the place he lived in.

Another example is Katsuya Toyoda, who admitted that his problem was not that he had a lot of things or more than the average person, but that there was not enough value in what was owned. Some of what he had, he did not like, but he only had it because it was part of a trend.

The idea behind Japanese minimalism and decluttering is about allowing what you love in your life. You do not have to focus on what is trendy or popular. Those who try to fit into the ideal, showing off what they have, will not necessarily be happy.

Minimalists have found that less materialistic thoughts give them more in life. As you journey through sections one and two, consider the ultimate question—what do you value in life? By the end, you will see that what you have put emphasis on in your life is not what you hold dearest in your heart; rather, it will be the people, family, and happiness that you learn to value above material items.

Your journey is not going to be quick. It is not an overnight transition but one that will take time. You actively have to change how you think before you can completely adopt the Japanese art of minimalism. Begin with small steps, take a few setbacks, and learn to discover what matters. In the end, you are going to find what has been missing all along from your life—true happiness, contentment, and lifelong friends.

4

SECTION I

Minimalism: The Starting Point

What is minimalism? What are the core values? What does it mean to live as a minimalist? These are the three questions to answer as you move through this first section. The answers might even surprise you. You are going to learn what the minimalist mindset is, the benefits, and how to transition from your current thoughts to the minimalist principles. Take as much time as you need with these three concepts before moving on to other topics. Use paper and pen or your computer to jot down details or to make your goal list. It is never too early to begin thinking about what you hope to gain by adopting the minimalist mindset.

6

Chapter 1

The Minimalist Mindset

Minimalism is a term you may hear often. Various artistic styles exist, such as Hygge (pronounced *Hooga*) and the Japanese art of minimalism. Each has its own set of rules to guide you toward a happier life. But, what is the basic definition of minimalism? What does it mean to have a minimalist mindset? To discover how you can lead a happier life at home and work, you desire answers to these questions and will undoubtedly have a few more as we work through this section.

According to the dictionary, minimalism is a word taken from the art world to define a trend in painting and sculpture that existed in the 1950s and also a movement in music in which short phrases gradually change. You might wonder why these two definitions matter when we are talking about decluttering your life. The idea behind the artistic movement and music was to have simplicity in the works, but still offer something of value to viewers and listeners.

If you think about minimalism as we define it around decluttering your life—it's the same concept. You are going to attempt to find simplicity in your life while you still have the things you value most.

To further understand the concept of minimalism, you have to examine the myths that surround it.

Minimalist Myths Debunked

When many people hear the term "minimalism," they think that it means they are not supposed to own anything, except what fits into a backpack. We are often taught to think this movement is unconventional, weird, and befitting of cults. There are many misconceptions about minimalism:

1. You do not have to sell your home and walk the earth tent camping.

2. Your possessions do not have to fit into a backpack.

3. Minimalism is about reducing what causes you worry, stress, and angst.

4. You do not have to be a part of a counterculture, cult, or commune.

5. Less is more, instead of less being uncomfortable.

The minimalist mindset focuses on what is important:

1. It is about reducing time spent on certain aspects of your life, when you want to have time to do more important things.

2. It is about leaving behind the material world trappings, where you feel you have to have something when you have no idea where you will even put it in your home.

3. Being in the right mindset allows you to have quality possessions.

4. You make sure you have quality friends around you.

5. You also gain an overall higher quality of life.

Recently, a webcast talked about self-publishing or traditional publishing, and the published author speaking discussed how she spent her time and how she marketed her self-published materials. The author outlined how everyday she wakes up early, completes three tasks per day toward marketing, and structures her life so that she can accomplish what matters. The answer was a step-by-step guide that implied to the listeners that focusing on these three tasks per day toward marketing, even if they only take five to ten minutes, is a way to get one's name out there. Now, this example may seem odd given our discussion on minimalism. But, think about it. If someone has a busy, cluttered life, and they cannot find the time for three marketing tasks, what would happen if they gained the minimalist mindset like the author has? By gaining quality over quantity, your life can become enhanced.

If you wish to make a better life for yourself or, if you have a family, for everyone, you need to consider what is important to you. Do you want to constantly spend time cleaning, decluttering things you do not use, and buying things, or instead, would you rather spend your life "doing" things?

The Minimalist Philosophy

Minimalists have certain traits in common. You do not need to adopt all nine of these points but consider what they mean and what you want from life.

1. Minimalists value their experiences over materialistic things.

2. Minimalists no longer buy items they do not need.

3. Minimalists become more diligent in who and what they allow in their life to avoid letting things overfill it again.

4. Time becomes a priority over physical items and shopping.

5. Minimalists have fewer things, so they do not have to spend time decluttering.

6. Minimalists' mindsets shift to realize happiness "comes from within," not from material items.

7. Minimalists leave behind the comparison to others and what they have, and that not only helps mentally but also financially. They are no longer trying to keep up.

8. Minimalists leave behind the fear of never having what they need. Instead of buying ten of something because they might need it someday, they buy only what they need now.

9. Organization is not the answer—less is.

You may have some of these traits, or you might need to figure out how to adopt them to discover your happiness. It is funny, but you will not even know the turning point in your life when you decide that you have found happiness. After striving to reduce your life to what matters most, one day you will wake up and realize your minimalist goal is accomplished.

It Is Not a Radical Lifestyle

Minimalism is not a radical lifestyle. If you are one of those who think, "I can never be a minimalist," then you need a moment to reconsider your opinion. It isn't a radical lifestyle, and you don't need to be a radical person to follow this lifestyle. In fact, a minimalist lifestyle isn't that much different from yours. You don't need to have a mental count of all the things you own, and you don't have to get rid of everything you own. However, there are a couple of things that distinguish a minimalist lifestyle.

Do You Believe in Excess?

The first distinction is that minimalists don't believe in excess. It means that you don't need anything else other than the things that you frequently use. It means that you need to get rid of all those 'just in case' items in your possession. Only keep things that add some value to your life. That being said, the definition of excess is subjective. For instance, if you want to be a globetrotting writer, then you can considerably reduce the number of things you own. However, if you are happy with where you live and don't plan to travel all the time, then you don't need to make these changes. If ever you decide to change your mind, then you can change things accordingly.

Do You Question Your Possessions?

Minimalists always question their possessions. There are a couple of simple questions that you can ask yourself to gauge your necessities. Do I really need this? When was the last time I used this thing? What will happen if I get rid of this? Does someone else need this more than I do? The beliefs of a minimalist constantly depend on these questions. The idea of minimalism is quite simple. A minimalist is in a constant state of paring down, and it does feel good. Minimalism is not a destination but an ongoing journey that doesn't end.

What Gives Meaning to Your Life?

A minimalist understands that it is not important to give any meaning to the possessions that he or she owns. A minimalist understands that possessions can be replaced. Everything that you own is pretty much replaceable. It is not a radical lifestyle but a tool to help remove all unnecessary things from your life. You can live a meaningful life when you strip away all the excess from life. It helps you concentrate on things that really matter, like relationships, health, passion, growth, and your contribution.

What about you? Can you strip away all the superficial things from your life and concentrate on the important things in life? Ask yourself these simple questions and you can decide if minimalism is meant for you.

Signs of a Minimalist

In this section, you will learn about the different signs of a minimalist.

Minimalists like to have order in every aspect of their life. Organizing is an important trait of minimalists. They either live an orderly life, or they aspire to live on. Do you like making lists, like to-do lists, shopping lists, grocery lists, or even guest lists? Do you like it when you can see your ideas and plans mapped out in front of you? Does it make you feel empowered? If you have a difficult task at hand, does it help when you make a plan to tackle it? Mess and disorder tend to turn you into a procrastinator (gasp)!

As a minimalist, you would like to look put together, always. You don't really fuss about your looks, but you do like to put your best foot forward. However, it doesn't mean that you dress up to the nines every time you need to step out of the house.

Your wardrobe consists of all those pieces and articles of clothing that express your personality and are made to last. A pair of jeans that fit you perfectly, a well-tailored jacket, the quintessential court shoes, a classic handbag, and a couple of other basic items are all you need to dress. You aren't crazy about any of the seasonal trends but instead, you like a wardrobe that is more of an investment and not a fad.

It doesn't mean that you cannot appreciate the finer things in life. You prefer quality to quantity and don't receive much satisfaction from any of the lesser substitutes. Fine quality and craftsmanship will always trump cheaper knockoffs. You probably prefer spending $300 dollars on a pair of Italian leather pumps that will last you a while instead of those $50 pretty-much-looks-the-same pair.

You don't like to waste things. It can be anything from your favorite lipstick to tissues in the kitchen. You vehemently dislike wastage.

Two things that appeal to you more than anything are cleanliness and functionality. Instead of decorative décor, you prefer something with even textures, neutral and subtle colors, and clean lines. If something doesn't have any functionality then you tend to avoid it. You value space when it comes to your home. You probably avoid furniture and fixtures that gobble up space and instead opt for things that make the home seem spacious and airy. The way you decorate your home is a mere extension of your personality.

When it comes to your finances, you are not a penny-pincher. However, it doesn't mean that you believe in the concept of living large. You don't hesitate to spend money on things that you love and the things that will last you a long time.

You don't deal well with clutter, and you hate it when there is clutter all around you. You prefer to simplify your life and continually reassess your possessions and priorities. Your dislike for clutter also extends to the people present in your life. You like to surround yourself with people who matter to you. The idea of quality over quantity is applicable to all aspects of your life.

If you exhibit any of the signs discussed in this section, then you are well on your way to becoming a minimalist.

TYPES OF MINIMALISTS

In the modern world, the word minimalism is infused with so many different meanings that it is difficult to understand if everyone is on the same page. The word is tossed around carelessly in conversations, and people seem to use it in different ways. Minimalism is an abstract concept, and there are different ways in which you can follow this concept. In this section, you will learn about the different types of minimalists. However, the common thread that binds all these different types of minimalists is the underlying philosophy of a lifestyle that's based on the idea of less.

Aesthetic Minimalists

For aesthetic minimalists, it is all about the optics. They might or might not own less, but they like to have fewer things on display. White is the go-to color for an aesthetic minimalist, and they like to incorporate this color in the aesthetics. It is quite easy to spot aesthetic minimalists. They like clean lines, neutral colors, and open spaces. So, if you walk through the front door and notice bare countertops, bare walls, and maybe even bare floors, then it is quite certain that you have walked into the house of an aesthetic minimalist.

Essential Minimalists

As the name suggests, essential minimalists like to stick to the bare essentials. They constantly try to see what the essential things in their lives are and what things they can live without. They like to use less and own less. Constantly paring down their belongings is an important trait of essential minimalists. Back to the basics seems to be the motto of essential minimalists. Quality and quantity do matter to them, but they absolutely detest wastage in any form. The essentialists don't horde things and will toss aside their old things to acquire some new ones. They do all this within their means and probably will not indulge in a purchase if there is no need for it.

Experiential Minimalists

Experiential minimalists tend to favor experiences over the pursuit to acquire things. So, experiential minimalists will own only a few possessions, and this is a symptom of their lifestyle and nothing else. Experiential minimalists can quintessentially fit their entire life into a backpack, and they will not have any qualms about it. This particular type of minimalist can include anyone, from an adventure-seeking traveler, a freelancing digital nomad, to a modern-day hippie.

Sustainable Minimalists

Sustainable minimalists are eco-minimalists. Their idea of life is to focus on eco-friendly living. They like the idea of reducing the dependence on things that harm the environment. They want to live a life that is sustainable for themselves and the environment. Eco-minimalists lead a homestead life or at least aspire to do so. This lifestyle is about not only serving the interests of the individual and their lifestyle but also the environment. The motto of an eco-minimalist is to "make do or do without." Sustainable minimalists use this motto to judge the necessity of things in their life.

Thrifty Minimalists

A minimalist detests wastage and thrifty minimalists hate it even more so. The waste-conscious habits of these minimalists are quite similar to that of the sustainable minimalists. However, the underlying intention that motivates these two categories of minimalists is quite different. Their idea is to reduce their spending and not to use less. Their financial mindset prompts them to embrace the minimalist lifestyle. Thrifty minimalists try to make do with whatever they have and try to limit their expenses as much as possible. They prefer to save, and the only thing that motivates them to do so is to reduce their financial expenditure.

Mindful Minimalists

Mindful minimalists derive joy and spiritual enlightenment whenever they get rid of extra things or unnecessary things from their life. Sensible moderation is their defining feature. The practice of moderation makes them happy and not for any environmental, financial, or aesthetic reasons. They do it for psychological reasons. Letting go of all materialistic possessions give mindful minimalists peace of mind. Peace of mind is something that is quite dear to this type of minimalist, and they try to maintain it at all times. Mindful minimalists strive to let go of all negative feelings that bog them down. Getting rid of all that is excess makes them more mindful and allows them to discover their purpose in life.

Well, these are the different types of minimalists. The fundamental philosophy that all minimalists agree on is their enthusiasm to get rid of excess and to make do with as little as possible. The reasons or motivations for doing so can differ.

Embrace the Minimalist Lifestyle

In this section, you will learn about the different ways in which you can incorporate minimalism into different aspects of your life.

Closets

Arranging or rearranging closets is a difficult chore. Most of us tend to hold on to clothes that we no longer wear or don't like. However, how many of us get rid of all these unnecessary items of clothing? In this section, you will learn about the way you can use minimalism to reorganize your closet.

You need to let go of all the items of clothing that are worn out. If something has holes in it and if you don't plan on wearing it immediately, then you need to get rid of it. If you haven't worn anything in a year, then you need to donate or sell those items of clothing as it is quite unlikely that you will start to wear it now. If something doesn't fit you well or you don't like the way it fits you, then you must sell or donate such clothes. They certainly don't belong in your closet.

How many clothes do you need? Do you really need to hold on to fifteen pairs of jeans when you keep repeating five pairs constantly?

You need to decide on a number, and you need to stick to that number. Once you decide, hold on to the exact number of hangers. For instance, if you decide that you need five pairs of trousers, five short-sleeved and five long-sleeved shirts, then you need fifteen hangers and no more than that. Go through all the items of clothing you own and select those that you cannot live without. While you do this, keep in mind that you can accommodate only a certain number of clothes and you need to stick to that limit.

You don't really need twenty-five pairs of shoes, do you? Select the pairs of shoes that you wear constantly and donate or sell the rest. Try to stick to the essentials and get rid of anything that seems like excess. Throw away all those socks and undergarments that look worse for the wear or have holes in them.

Kitchen

The kitchen is an important room in any home. Here are some tips that will help you reorganize your kitchen.

If you notice that there are some dishes that are chipped or cracked, then you need to remove them. You don't need fifty coffee mugs in the house, do you? Keep one mug per person and a few extra ones for any guests. Other than that, you can throw the rest away or donate them to a thrift store. If you have any appliances or kitchen gadgets that you don't use, then you need to give those away or discard them. If you have a food processor that you don't use daily but use a couple of times a month, you can hold on to it. If you have a kitchen appliance that you used once and then forgot all about, then you need to get rid of it. You need to throw away all duplicates. If you have multiple sets of measuring cups, keep one and let go of the rest. One method is to clear out one portion of the kitchen after the other and replace it with only those items that you absolutely need and cannot live without.

If you have any pre-packaged food at home, check the expiry date and dispose of it accordingly. There is no point in holding on to expired canned goods, is there? If any food item has expired, then throw it in the bin. If there are any broken appliances, utensils, or dishes, please throw them away.

Toys

If you have children at home, then you need to apply the ideals of minimalism even to the toys that they own. If there are any toys that your children don't play with weekly, then you need to get rid of those toys. If your children are old enough, then you can let them decide. If anything is broken, then you need to discard it. If the children have outgrown their toys and games, then you can donate or sell such toys. Pick toys that don't need a lot of storage space. Whenever you purchase something for your children, always opt for quality and not quantity. If your children have a lot of stuffed animals, then you can keep a few and discard the rest. It is a good idea to donate all the toys that your children no longer need.

Bathroom

Only keep the toiletries that you use, and don't keep a whole lot of extras just lying around. If you don't use it, then you don't need it. Check the medicine cabinet and get rid of all those expired medicines that you have. You can even call the local county government to dispose of all the expired medicines. You need a few towels and a couple of extras. You certainly don't need to go overboard with towels and hand towels in your bathroom. If you have some makeup that you don't use or if it has expired, then you need to replace it all. If there are some appliances like hair dryers, trimmers, shavers, or straightening or curling irons that you no longer use, then it is time to remove them.

Living Area

Don't let clutter into your living room. You need to follow the idea of minimalism here as well. Everyone tends to have a collection of movie and music cases. However, in the digitized world that we live in, you can easily get rid of all these cases and simply use the internet to watch a movie. After all, we are living in the world of Netflix. Do you really think you need those old movie cases? It is a good idea to digitize your movies and music. You can always store all that you like in a hard drive and avoid cluttering up the living area. If you have certain books that you don't like, or you don't read, then please donate them. Almost all books are digitally available these days. So, why not make the most of technology? You also need to decrease the number of knick-knacks you have in the house. Unless the collectibles have some sentimental or emotional value, you need to get rid of them.

These are just a couple of ways in which you can embrace the minimalist lifestyle. It is a constant work in progress, and you need to work on it. Try to donate things that you no longer use. If you do, you will feel good about yourself.

How to Live a Minimalist Life

You might think that a minimalist lifestyle is not for everyone. However, in the hectic world that we live in, most people yearn to spend less, to do less, and to need a little less. If you want to do any of these things, then minimalism is the answer to all your problems. In this section, you will learn about different steps that you can take to live a minimalist life.

A Goal

You need a clear, personal goal and a timeline. According to you, what is the definition of a minimalist lifestyle? Does it mean that you need to have only the bare minimum? Does it mean that you need to declutter your home? Does it mean to learn to live with what you have and stop buying things? Well, there is no right or wrong definition of minimalism. The concept of minimalism is subjective, and it can differ from one person to another. Take a moment or two and define what minimalism means for you. If you are not sure how you can make a list of things that you don't want in life, then you should simply make a list of things that you do want. List down the things that make you happy, make you feel alive, and that you are passionate about. Once you do this, you can then start to discard everything else that doesn't meet any of the above-mentioned points.

Set a clear goal for yourself. Once you set a goal, the next step is to simplify this goal into simple and easy to attain steps. You need to write down your goal and then make a list of steps that you can take to achieve your goal. Once you do this, the next step is to establish a timeline for each of the steps you listed

Your Home

A smaller or a simplified home will take you a step closer to your goal of minimalism. If you own or rent a home, this can be a major lifestyle change. However, it is not an impossible thing to achieve. You need to think about your goal and be specific. You aren't sure what you want? Then do some research, travel a little, and take a look at the kind of house that matches your idea of minimalism. Minimalism doesn't necessarily mean that you need to downsize, it simply means that you need to hold on to the things that you need and discard everything else.

Declutter

You need to declutter. It is an obvious step but can be quite difficult for all those people who tend to have an attachment to most of the things they own. You need to start slow. It is a conscious decision. Discard or donate all the things that you don't need. The first step of decluttering is to remove the obvious items that you don't use. You can then store everything else that you think you can do without for a couple of months. It will give you the time to not only distance yourself from these things but will also help you gauge their importance. You might think that if you don't need something and get rid of it, you will later realize that perhaps that item wasn't as insignificant to you as you initially assumed. Instead of throwing everything away, try to slowly transition yourself. You need some motivation and courage to declutter. You need to remind yourself time and again that your goal is to lead a minimal lifestyle and anything that doesn't help further the goal needs to go. It doesn't mean that you need to live a Spartan life. Remember, your idea of minimalism might not be the same as someone else. You need to decide what a minimal lifestyle means to you and proceed accordingly.

Train Yourself

If you are a creature of comfort, then it will take you a while before you can adapt to the minimal lifestyle. Give yourself a couple of weeks or months, and then you can slowly start to eliminate all the unnecessary comforts and luxuries. It can be something as simple as forgoing a pricey haircut or extravagant meals. Keep the things that make you happy. Don't hold on to things because you are used to having them around.

Question

A question that you need to ask yourself constantly is "Do I need this?" Whenever you make a purchase, think about whether you need it or not. You must be able to distinguish between a want and a need. Food, clothing, shelter, security, and love are needs. Everything else is a want. At first, it is quite likely that you will try to justify all your purchases. Did you watch *The Confessions of a Shopaholic?* In this movie, Isla Fischer has a hard time resisting the urge to purchase things. She cannot distinguish between a want and a need. Her inability to do this makes her quite miserable and also bankrupt. So, the next time you decide to purchase something because it appeals to you, take a moment and think, "Do I really need this?"

Reuse

Learn to reuse. If you want to live a minimal life, then you need to start reusing. Learn to repair or fix things instead of replacing them. For instance, you can fashion old glass bottles into flower vases. You can use old fabric for DIY projects. A simple Google search will help you find easy DIY projects that will help you avoid making any unnecessary purchases. Find creative ways to reuse things around your house, instead of purchasing things. Reusing will help you save money and reutilize all those things that you were about to throw away. However, it doesn't mean that you start to horde things.

There is a fine line between hoarding and reusing. You need to learn to make a distinction between these two.

Quality

Always opt for quality over quantity. If you do want to splurge on something, then it makes sense to splurge on a good-quality item. A couple of good-quality items are more meaningful than a whole bunch of cheap-quality products that will only last you a month or two.

Clarity

You need to revisit the first step constantly. It means that you need to have clarity about what minimalism means to you. It will help you focus on your goals and not get distracted.

If you want to become a minimalist, then you need to learn to be patient with yourself. It is a significant lifestyle change but also requires you to change the way you think. It will take a while and don't expect to see a change overnight. Not just that, but there will be instances where you might slip up. The thing that you need to remember is to forgive yourself and keep going. That's the only way that you will learn to become a minimalist. The trick is to keep going and not give up.

Chapter 2

Benefits of Minimalism

Becoming a minimalist provides opportunities that you have been missing before. Each benefit ties into each other, so it is not that you work toward one, but rather that you gain them all as you declutter. Some benefits may come more easily to you depending on how ready you are to accept the minimalist mindset. Other benefits may not be as essential to your life as certain gains listed. Think through the mindset and the benefits to decide your starting point and your goal.

Freedom

Freedom can be described regarding financial and personal peace. It also relates to being freer to do the things you love.

Being materialistic can hamper you. You tend to buy things, even if there is no clear reason. You might think, "Perhaps that will go well on the mantle" or "I have space for a new picture on the wall." These tendencies prevent us from being free to enjoy the things we love.

From a financial perspective, hobbies and travel are expensive. If you spend $3, $6, or $10 here and there or every day, you compromise affording hobbies and travel. Consider the coffee dilemma. Let's say you work near a place that offers you $3 drinks, whether it is a coffee, latte, chai latte or tea. You work four days a week. Each day you work, you buy a $3 chai latte, which means you spend $12 per week. You spend $48 per month. At the end of the year, you have spent $576 on chai lattes.

Now consider a warehouse store. At one store you can spend $7.98 for ninety-six fluid ounces of chai. A twenty-ounce chai latte is ten ounces of chai and ten ounces of milk. You will get about ten days of chai lattes from a purchase at a warehouse store. You could even decide to go with five ounces of chai per drink versus ten to get twenty days of chai . If you only drink it four times a week, then you have five weeks' worth of chai lattes. What could you do with the savings? You could fly to a new destination. You could spend that money on your hobby. You could pay off a debt that is worrisome. Above all, you could gain financial freedom to do more of the things you love.

Time is another factor of freedom. What if you need to keep working to afford the credit card payments? Some jobs offer paid time off for vacations, but if you keep spending money can you afford to go? You may figure out that you need a second source of income versus a holiday to pay off your debts.

Your time may also be filled with shopping and other time-consuming tasks preventing you from feeling free. Minimalism is not just about materialistic items but also about how much of your time is filled with useless or unnecessary tasks.

Keep freedom and time in mind as you read about other benefits.

Worry-Free Living

Spending money causes stress. Agonizing over the things you cannot afford to do or do not have time for can eat away at you. Minimalizing your life gives you the opportunity to have peace of mind. You will become less stressed and worried because you are decluttering your life of the trappings that make you fearful.

What is causing you to worry now? Are you wondering where you will come up with the next mortgage payment? Is your credit card debt over $10,000, maybe closer to $30,000? Do you wonder how you will get one child to their extra-curricular activity without making your other child late?

Maybe you look around your home and think, "When will I have the time to organize and clean?" You might look at a book you want to read and have no idea when you can do something for yourself like read that book.

Stress is something we create for ourselves, so if we adopt a minimalist lifestyle, we can let go of the worry and stress. We can make peace with the things we cannot do as a way to enjoy the things that are possible.

You cannot buy peace of mind, but you can attain it through minimalism and live a happier life.

Health

When you are stress-free and you gain time for yourself, your health improves. Health is a mental and physical concept. Physically, your health gets better when you put more focus into exercising, eating correctly, and getting rid of debilitating habits. Mentally, you gain health because you are worry free. Your fear and stress dissipate.

What would you do if you had an hour to yourself? If you didn't worry about cleaning, where the kids need to go next, or how to pay a bill? How free would you feel? Studies show the minimalist lifestyle improves health because you can relax, unwind, and focus on what is most essential—your health.

Focus

How well are you focusing when you have a million tasks? We like to think we can multi-task, but what we do is switch-task, not always finishing something before moving on. Can you type on a computer and talk at the same time? Try it. Did you just type something you said versus the thought you meant to type? Of course, because you are trying to split your focus. When you have less to think about, you have more focus on the tasks at hand.

Our brains can compartmentalize to sharpen our focus. When you are at work—doing your best—do you bring your personal life with you? No, you cannot for fear of losing your job. You have to leave your worries behind and get the work accomplished. Decluttering your life allows you to do this. You have fewer worries, you find more time, and your health is better; therefore, you can focus more on what matters most to you and the tasks you need to complete.

Less Fear of Failure

Fear of failure comes from having too much to do and no time or focus to make it happen. You see how each of these benefits ties into one another? They do not tie in a linear way, but in multiple pathways. By restructuring your life, you not only gain freedom, a less stressful experience, and more focus, but you also do not have to fear the consequences.

What if you:

- Put your entire monthly income toward your debts, groceries, mortgage, and utilities;

- Have no money left for fun;

- Are left with debts that are more than you can pay each month;

- End up in foreclosure and bankruptcy.

This what-if statement is just an example of what you might consider a lifetime failure. Other fears can include failing your children or your spouse, or to obtain the goals you have. When your mind is full of worry, you lack proper health, and you have no time for yourself or others, you feel like a failure. But, you do not have to feel this way. Leave all of these thoughts behind by minimizing the things in life you don't need and go after what is essential.

Decluttering

A step toward minimalism is decluttering. You streamline your life to fit your goals. You get rid of things that you have not used in the last six months. You buy only what is necessary. In your home you can gain more room, or you can downsize to a smaller, less worrisome home. In this way, you lower your carbon footprint in the world.

Regaining Values

The last benefit to discuss deals directly with the larger world problems. There is a general shift in thought with people thinking they are entitled from the moment they are born. They are entitled to own huge properties, earn $100,000 a year, and have vacations. But, are you?

Let's consider values throughout history. Yes, some individuals took property and goods through legal means, such as fighting to overtake someone else's property. Some religious people stole money in the name of their religion and used that money for their gain and not to help others. But, despite the bad deeds of some people, the majority of people understood that to have anything you must work for it.

This is still true today. It might take twenty years to earn vacation for someone. For another person, they may live paycheck to paycheck but are happier than the person who consistently makes more but never has anything to show for it besides material items.

By regaining values and realizing that if you work hard, you will be happy and gain what is essential to you, your life will improve. The minimalist mindset teaches us to discover our values.

Chapter 3

The Transition

At this juncture, you think you can become a minimalist. The benefits sound wonderful, and you want to live a happier, freer life. But, how can you transition from the habits and lifestyle you have to the minimalist one?

There are numerous answers to the above question. Not one of the answers is the "right" one. Each person has to transition in a way that makes the most sense to them. You might look at the twenty-one--day steps that are outlined below and know you can keep to the schedule, but what happens after? Are you the type of person that can continue on that minimalism path even if you encounter problems?

A key element to transitioning into the minimalist mindset is knowing your strengths and weaknesses. Courtney Carver believes there are three types of categories new minimalists fit into. But, you cannot quantify it to just three because everyone has a personality, separate from the rest of the world. We are individuals because of these traits. Do not think you have to conform to Carver's three categories.

The first category is the person ready to go, ready to become a minimalist and declutter their home. The second is the type of person who feels they have limited space, not that they have too much to fill the space they have. The third is interested but does not know how to begin the process.

The law of averages says a person who rushes into decisions will falter at some point during the process. The individual who takes their time, thinks it through, and slowly begins to become a minimalist often succeeds where others do not. Again, there is no hard and fast rule about how you change your life and adopt the Japanese art of minimalism. Do what works for you, correct the transition process if something does not work, and realize that you may have to work at it for a while.

Minimalism is a lifestyle change, not an overnight transition.

This is the point where you need to assess reality.

- Do you have a spouse?

- Do you have children?

- Are there other family members who are part of your life or that you live with?

- Do you take a radical change with ease or does it cause fear?

- Are you willing to experiment before you find the level of minimalism you are comfortable with?

- Do you know what makes you happy?

- Are you willing to accept that you will continue to try and define your life, so there is no end point to reach with minimalism?

How you answer the above questions is going to define what you are willing to try and do to become a minimalist. For people who have a spouse, the husband or wife will need to accept your need to change and have less to gain more. If children are involved, then you are teaching them a lesson, but a drastic change may not be possible.

Children learn from their parents. Seeing an extravagant lifestyle that is suddenly reduced to a few favorite things, with fewer expensive vacations or presents, will result in a need for time to adjust. But, the good news is you can teach them better values as you make this transition and help them see why you felt a change was necessary.

Seven Possible Steps

The following are seven suggestions you might consider to begin the transition of becoming a minimalist.

- Write down a plan based on reality.

- Find one place in your home that is clutter-free. This is the room that never becomes a mess. It is the room to start with, and then you can eventually make other rooms just as clutter-free.

- Get rid of duplicate items, whether it is clothing or photographs.

- Dress using less clothing and alternate how you wear them in combination.

- Travel with fewer items. Do you need a bathing suit each day you are in the Caribbean? Are you going to need more than three changes of clothes for a week on a cruise, when you have a way to wash them? You can travel with less.

- Adapt the meals you eat, such as using the crockpot more, as making meals that contain all nutritional value with fewer steps is possible. You can simplify meals to gain more time with family.

- Save at least $1,000. This is the end step in this process of transition. You can do this by changing your shopping habits for clothing, new home items, and food. When you are buying less, it is possible to save more.

You may be a person that needs more steps or more elaborate considerations. You may also need a plan that is less easy to forget about.

Discover Twenty-One Steps

Psychologists believe that your mind needs twenty-one days to form new habits. To break the cycle you are in, you want to make certain your brain can adapt. This idea can also be applied to becoming a minimalist with a twenty-one step plan done over a period of twenty-one days to help your brain restructure. You may need longer. You might require less time. But, if you want to feel less stress, more confidence, and overall success, then trying for a twenty-one-day change is helpful. Better than anything else, you can use this concept for dieting, meal planning, and minimalism, so it is not just a concept rooted solely in changing your mindset to be a minimalist.

1. Decide to become a minimalist.

2. Plan your steps to make this happen.

3. Start packing what you know you do not need.

4. Organize the essential items.

5. Assess the things that give you pause—you might have a sentimental attachment but can still get rid of it.

6. Examine the fear you feel for your new lifestyle.

7. Look at the relationships in your life and who is helping you.

8. Believe that changes can be made.

9. Grow as a person.

10. Examine everything so far and see how you feel.

11. Get rid of the trash.

12. Start selling items to others who will value them.

13. Donate what cannot be sold.

14. Digitize aspects of your life to declutter, such as photographs.

15. Examine what is left and continue reducing what you can.

16. Target your car—can you get rid of it or own a more minimalist vehicle?

17. Can you move to a smaller home?

18. What can you change at work to declutter and minimalize?

19. Are there areas of your health you can target?

20. Do you have too many electronics? Can you change how you watch TV?

21. Now you have more time. Organizing and decluttering your life has just provided you with TIME. How will you enjoy it?

These twenty-one steps help you rethink your current life. They allow you to consider the possibilities and make a move toward a happier lifestyle. But, they are not set in stone. You might begin digitizing your photographs before you decide to trash things. Make your transition plan based on who you are, your strengths, and your current commitments.

Your Psychology

What type of personality do you have? Do you think you do better with a few guidelines or every step written out? When you transition into the minimalist mindset, you must know who you are.

Take a look at your life as it is now. What if you were given six months to move out of your home? What if you had to move four times in three years? A lot of times when you look at a situation with a different perspective, it is easier to see how you can become a minimalist, but do you start regaining things in your life once it begins to settle down?

One family has dealt with several struggles in a short period of five years. It started with a move due to health issues, which turned into four moves in three years for one of the family members. Another went through a bankruptcy, divorce, and two years of a battle over children simply for one parent to "win" against the other. Now this family faces another move, with six months to make it happen. For some people, their strength may be gone, but for others, it is the time where each family member rallies to ensure the best possible outcome.

You never know what you will do until you are faced with a situation. If you need something enough, you will find a way to make it happen.

So, begin your transition by assessing what your life has been like, how it has shaped you, and the potential changes you can gain.

What is the hardest event in your life that you have had to face? There is no right or wrong answer. For one person, it might be the loss of a pet, and for another person, it is wondering if this is the year he or she will become paralyzed due to genetic health disorders.

When you faced that difficult event, how did you handle it? Looking back, were there things you could have done better? Going back to the example of the family above, the wife and her two children had to face losing the male of their household. The wife lost a spouse and the children lost a father too early due to onset dementia. One adult child could not be there due to a troubled marriage and two children. The other child never thought she had enough strength to watch her father die slowly, day by day. The wife was not going to leave his side, but she got lost in the loss, unable to focus on anyone else's loss of this same person.

We all react differently to major life events, and, because they are the most trying, they also tell us the most about our personality. You may think you have hit rock bottom until yet another thing tries to strike you down, and you realize life is not all that bad because there are things you still value.

The point is, you will need to assess who you are to know your current limitations and discover your true limits as you work toward a minimalist lifestyle. Right now, you may think, "I do not know how to transition" or "How can I keep to this schedule if something else happens?" The answer is that you will find it when you get to that point.

The move into a minimalist lifestyle is as much about the journey as it is about meeting the goals you set.

If you can remember the above statement, then you can transition to a new lifestyle based on your current psychological traits. You will learn more about yourself as you begin your journey. Look forward to the coming changes.

Embrace what you discover.

You are ready for the next section. You are prepared to start the practical application of the concepts that will move you into a minimalist lifestyle. Be strong, get back up and on track when you falter, and enjoy journeying through minimalism to reach your goals. You are capable of making an impact.

Chapter 4

What Matters the Most to You?

The primary focus of minimalism is to hold on to the things that are important to you and to let go of everything else. However, how do you decide what is important and what isn't?

Minimalism + Goal Setting

Do you like the idea of minimalism but aren't certain where to begin? Well, one of the reasons why a lot of people want to try minimalism is because of the overwhelming lifestyles we lead these days, as minimalism can help make it more manageable. The first thing that you need to do if you want to start with minimalism is understanding where to start. Only when you know where to start will you be able to create helpful habits.

If your goal is to simplify, then you need to understand that a relation exists between physical and emotional clutter. When you start to remove physical clutter from your surroundings, you need to concentrate on getting rid of emotional clutter as well. There are four steps you can use when you want to set a goal for yourself.

Step One: Identify Your goal

The first step is to identify your goal and determine the manner in which it relates to your overall lifestyle. Identify the reasons why a goal is important for you and prepare for the journey toward minimalism. If you don't set a goal for yourself, then it is quite likely that you will not make any real progress. You might even make some half-hearted attempts to try minimalism, but without a goal, you will not make any progress. Minimalism is not a restrictive lifestyle, but it is a tool that will help you live a fuller life.

Step Two: Don't Hold Yourself Back

Most of us tend to keep making new goals while not achieving our old goals. Do you declare a goal whenever you make one? However, after a while, do you forget about it and move on to something else? If yes, then you need to take a moment and think about all the instances in the past where you made a goal but did not achieve it. You need to avoid all those mistakes. Think about all the factors that were holding you back and try working around them instead. There are two major factors that prevent you from achieving your goal.

The first factor is perfectionism, and the second one is self-doubt or self-acceptance. The idea of perfection is an alluring illusion. Most of us tend to waste our time chasing perfection. In fact, there is nothing in this world that is perfect, and the more you try to chase it, the more elusive it will seem. Take a moment and breathe. Perfectionism will prevent you from taking any action. Instead of trying to perfect something, just take some action. Any action is better than sitting and wondering whether it will be perfect or not.

You need to learn to accept yourself. If you want to change something, then the first step is acceptance. Have you seen a rocking chair? A little momentum and it doesn't stop to rock. Well, stress is pretty much like a rocking chair. It will give you something to think about, but it doesn't get you anywhere good. Familiarity brings comfort, and it is easy. On the other hand, the unknown is quite scary. When you learn to let go and accept where you are in life, it becomes easier to deal with the outcome. Change doesn't have to be wrong; think of it as an adventure. Even those who seem quite confident get a little scared from time to time. Whenever you start to worry about what the future will be like, you need to remind yourself that no one can predict the future. You never know what might come your way. There are times when you imagine the absolute worst but the outcome isn't that bad, and vice versa. So, accept that you must live in the present and let destiny do its work.

You need to be confident about yourself. Don't try to indulge in superficial things to mask any self-doubt that you feel. Learn to accept yourself and understand that materialistic things are merely a small part of life. Your attitude toward yourself will determine your attitude toward things.

Step Three: Visualization

Visualize the big picture. This step goes together with the first step. You need to visualize what success looks like to you. You need to be as descriptive as you possibly can be. Talk to yourself about how great it will feel when you achieve the goal. The clearer and more detailed your visualization, the more motivated you will feel to achieve that goal.

Step Four: Plan of Action

Once you have a goal in mind, the next step is to have a plan of action. A goal without a plan of action to achieve it is merely a dream. If you don't want your goal to be just a dream, then you need to create a plan to achieve your goal. Your effort determines the outcome. So, you need to motivate yourself even when you feel like giving up. A plan helps you focus and use your energy according to the priorities you set for yourself.

If you want to set goals for yourself to achieve minimalism, then you need to follow the simple steps discussed in this chapter.

Self-Assessment

If you don't know what is important to you, then make a list of things that you do love. Minimalism isn't about cutting things out of your life or creating a void. Instead, minimalism is about holding on to what matters to you. The first goal of minimalism is to identify the things that are essential to you and then discard all other things. We overburden ourselves with physical and emotional clutter. This clutter can easily make you feel overwhelmed and quite lost in life. Not just that, but all the excess that we surround ourselves with distracts us from our goals, and we tend to do things that don't really matter. If you don't want to live like this anymore, then you need to think about minimalism. Socrates once said, "The unexamined life is not worth living." Well, this saying stands true, now more than ever. If you want to simplify your life, then you need to examine your life. There are some questions that you need to ask yourself to understand your needs.

Question #1

The first question that you need to ask yourself is: "What do I love the most?" or "What means the most to me?" The answer to this question will obviously be different for different people. In fact, there is no right or wrong answer. For some, it might mean to spend quality time with their family, reading a book, cooking, or even traveling. Before you can decide about minimalism, the first thing that you need to do is decide what is important to you.

Question #2

The next question that you need to ask yourself is about all the things that you do on a daily basis and the manner in which they relate to the previous question. So, ask yourself, "What are the different things that are going on in my life, and how do these things relate to what matters to me?" For instance, you may go out for drinks with your friends at least once a week, but you really don't think it's important. Then, in such a case, you simply need to stop doing it. You can concentrate on something else instead. Take some time and think about all your commitments, and try to understand those that matter and those that don't.

Question #3

Think about all of your possessions. Ask yourself whether you love everything you own or not. Do you really love all your possessions? Are all your possessions important? There is another simple way in which you can determine whether you love something or not. For instance, if your house burns down, what are the things that you can replace? The answer to this question will help you understand the things that matter to you. You can simply get rid of all the other things. All that you are left with are the possessions that you value. Get rid of all the clutter. Clutter prevents you from enjoying the things that you love.

Question #4

You can use the same logic that you used to determine what possessions were important to you to determine the value of everything else in your life. For instance, you are probably surrounded by a lot of people daily. However, in your time of need, whom do you depend on? The ones that you depend on are the ones that you truly love. The rest are mere acquaintances. It is okay to have a handful of dependable and trustworthy friends instead of a long list of fair-weather friends and frenemies.

Question #5

Where do you spend most of your time? What do you spend most of your time on? You can use these questions as a yardstick to determine the things that matter to you. Do you spend a lot of your time reading, watching TV, working on your laptop, or with your spouse? People do matter a lot. However, there are other things that are equally important as well. The time that you invest in something determines its importance.

Question #6

Where do you spend your money? What do you spend your money on? You perhaps buy clothes, travel, or invest. You can determine the importance of an aspect of your life based on your spending habits.

Question #7

What do you think about? For instance, if you are just sitting by yourself, then what do you think about? Do you think about something or someone? Your thoughts can also help you determine the importance of a particular aspect of your life. Wherever your thoughts drift, your heart goes along.

Question #8

If you have one day to live, then how will you spend your day? For instance, if today is the last day of your life, what will you do? Your mind will automatically think about the things that you value the most. The areas or aspects of your life that you don't think about aren't that important.

Question #9

What makes you happy? If you aren't able to come up with a conclusive answer even after answering all the previous questions, then this question might give you some clarity. There can be one or multiple reasons for your answer.

What are you left with? Once you answer the previous questions, you will be left with things that are important to you. You will finally have the answer to the question "What matters the most?" If you can get rid of all the distractions and unnecessary things, then you can finally start to concentrate on the things that do matter.

Phillip Lark

SECTION II

Declutter: The Art of Tidying Up

You have reached the practical section of joining others who have adopted the Japanese art of minimalism. The information you learn here is geared toward decluttering your life so that you can enjoy the minimalist lifestyle you are eager to begin. You will find practical tips and suggestions in the following chapters. Once you learn what decluttering means, you are going to find there are plenty of methods to streamline your life toward the goals you set in the last section. Here is where you will take the transitional steps, apply them through decluttering, and feel happier. You can accomplish anything you set your mind to, including getting out of the cycle you are currently in of adopting to the latest trends. Your new lifestyle is just beginning; and remember—you can modify your goals and journey as it best fits with who you are and who you want to be.

54

Chapter 5

A Life without Clutter is a Happy Life

Decluttering is a process you can use in your day-to-day life and at work. It is also a part of adopting and adapting to the minimalist mindset. In section one, you learned minimalism is about having what matters to you, which means less materialistic trappings. Decluttering is the method for streamlining your life, work and emotions. Decluttering is going to include assessing your house, digital life, emotions, and work. You will discover throughout your journey that you do not need to have as many things around you to be happy. It will work out that you want to have less, once you start the process of tidying up.

There are a couple of things you will need to keep in mind as you assess your life and work situations. The key question successful minimalists ask is whether something holds value. We are not talking about cash value, but a more meaningful value. Objects can be priceless to you and junk to someone else. The art of tidying includes taking a hard look at what you own and how much time it consumes from your life.

Your life can be discussed in three different categories and a few subcategories. The three main categories are your work life, your personal life, and your emotions. You have a personal life and a work life. Work is about making an income and being valued for your talents. It gives you a reason for why you wake up in the morning beyond just living. Your personal life is everything else—the house you keep, children, digital belongings, and emotions. Of course, you have work emotions too, which is why emotions is its own category that can be discussed beyond your personal life. You also need to keep your emotions out of your work life, and vice versa. The best employees keep their emotions to a minimum at work to ensure they are working effectively and not overstepping. For these reasons, we are going to discuss the three categories as new sections under the art of tidying up.

Personal Life

When you declutter your personal life with an eye toward minimalism, you focus on three subcategories: your house, your digital life, and your relationships.

House

A lot of myths about minimalism have people thinking it is about decluttering and reducing their home. But, it does not have to be about that. It is just one aspect. Since your house is just a portion of your personal life, it will be examined from a rational standpoint versus one of sentimentality.

Let's say you have a home that is 256 square feet. As a tiny house, you can have the entire thing, including the inside of the cabinets and the floors, mopped in an hour. What if your home is 2,560 square feet? If it takes an hour to do under 300 feet, going from the ceiling to the floor, inside and out of cabinets, then it would take ten hours to do a thorough clean on 2,560 square feet. Perhaps you remember as a kid having to clean the house on Saturday, with the help of your family, and you would be lucky to finish by noon because your home was around 3,000 square feet? When you have a family to help you the cleaning goes faster, but if only you were cleaning it, it would take you many long hours.

Not only that, but you have to do a regular cleaning every one to two weeks depending on the pets in the family. If you have dogs or cats, then you need to clean at least once a week. Imagine if you spend four hours each week doing the floors in the rooms you use, cleaning cat or dog fur from the couches, dusting the obvious areas, and getting the spatter off the kitchen counters, cabinets, and stove. In a year, there are fifty-two weeks. You would spend 208 hours cleaning.

Now, think about how often you clean and how you can cut down the time it takes? There is a way to spend less time cleaning—you get rid of the pets, you cut the clutter, and then you save time. Of course, you love your pets, so how about just getting rid of the clutter in your home? If you do not have to tidy up every time you clean, you will save time.

The amount of time taking care of your home takes out of your day is directly related to the amount of stuff you have. It continually needs cleaning, and with clutter, it will always need organizing. The larger the space and the more you have to fill it, the more time it takes. Your house, if you own it, requires upkeep, maintenance, and repairs.

We are taught if we have a large house, we must fill it with stuff. We tend to keep finding new things to bring home until eventually, we have too much.

Decluttering helps you purge the items you never use, reduce your wardrobe, and gain time to focus on what matters.

Once you complete this task, you may discover your home is too large and you are too inclined to fill it again.

The minimalist mindset will start, and you will think about the downsizing—how much space do you need?

A claustrophobic person with plenty of windows and less than 300 square feet can live happily, as long as they are not sharing the space with anyone else. What studies are showing as the minimalist movement grows and tiny homes are more popular is that a family of four needs 100 square feet of space that is all theirs. There is also the need for family rooms and kitchen, which require no more than 200 square feet for comfortable living. It means a family of four can survive and have space to relax away from family in 500 to 600 square feet.

If you are not convinced of this, do a test. Plenty of tiny homes are available for a short rental. You can see if you miss any of the clutter, disorganization, and space you have in your home during the short stay in a tiny home. You might find there are quite a few things you can live without.

Another way to look at your home and how much you have to fill it up is whether you would move away from that place or how many times you would be willing to move something. The more you move the same things often enough, the more you want them gone. In the previous section, you learned about an example where someone moved four times in three years. Imagine having to schlep the same number of boxes every time this person moved. When you encounter difficult moves, you begin to reassess what is most important about your life.

Decluttering, minimalizing, and then organizing what is left quickly becomes an easily adopted skill set. In your home, decluttering is going to mean removing the items you do not need, organizing what is left, and making sure everything has its place. The next challenge is making sure you put those things away when you come home, instead of throwing them on a table somewhere.

Digital

Our digital lives explode. Decluttering your digital life helps you streamline all aspects of your personal affairs. Do you need the hundreds of photos saved to the Cloud? Do you need every file saved on your computer? Do you need as many computers and digital devices as you have? Are there things you can store as digital files to get rid of the physical clutter in your home?

The essential question is what do you do with it all? When you get to the method of decluttering, ask yourself the question, and if the answer is not good enough, solve the problem with decluttering.

Consider for a moment how many times you have gone to the same place with your camera. How many of those pictures did you upload to your social media or print out for someone? If a picture is not used on social media, why keep it? If you have not printed it out, why keep it? Have you looked at a file you started five years ago about planning a vacation that you went on two years ago? These are the types of questions you will start asking yourself when you get to the digital concept of decluttering. For now, they are ideas to help get you thinking about why you need to tidy up more than just your home when it comes to your personal life.

Relationships

There are two types of relationships - the people you must associate with and those you choose to include in your life. The family is difficult to cut ties with; however, you can lessen your exposure. For emotional health, you may need to spend less time with family, but you cannot completely ignore them. Even if you live miles apart and in another state, there are times you will need to interact with your family. They are just a part of your personal life.

Family, what can you do with them? There is something divorced people learn when they have kids: you are never rid of that spouse, no matter how much you wish to be. You have to put up with certain things in your life because of family. It is not fun, fair, or always a way to declutter, but you can minimalize your situation.

1. Put distance between you and your family, if possible.

2. If you live too close, work on your mental health. What is it about that family member? Is there abuse in your relationship? Do you need that person to think of you as a grown up and they do not? Your mental health will improve once you admit there are two sides to every situation, and the answer is in the middle.

For example, a mother and daughter have a decent relationship. They have been friends, but there are still feelings that are difficult to address. The daughter often went to her father for advice and felt the mother put the eldest child, a son, first. It turns out that the mother emphasized her relationship with the son for two reasons, namely that the daughter was self-sufficient and more independent. It was a personality trait of independence that had the mother focusing on the one that needed more confidence, help, and care. It didn't mean the daughter didn't require some hands-on care, but the way the daughter asked and the admittance of that need didn't always make it clear to the mother. The point is you can repair certain family relationships, and for those you cannot, like if the issue is emotional abuse, you can still work through your stressors to declutter your emotions and live happier.

When it comes to relationships that are not family, such as friends, you get to decide. Friends who cause harm and do not support you can be "decluttered." You do not have to keep toxic relationships if they plague you. It is hard, but solutions exist. Later, when we get to the practical tips of decluttering, you are going to learn how you can minimalize the people you have in your life.

For now, let's say you have friends you trust, but they often enable behavior you are trying to change. Your resolve becomes nil in their presence. You can distance yourself. You can decide that until you can say "no," you are not going to be around this friend, but you will at least continue to talk with them.

Any toxic relationship needs to end. How it ends is up to you and the issues that exist. A toxic marriage that ends in divorce may still require contact with the toxic issues, but you can again minimalize how affected you are by compartmentalizing, relaxing the trouble, and knowing there is no changing it. You cannot be responsible for someone else and their behavior. You must step back. It is easier said than done.

1. Limit communications.

2. Communicate your thoughts and end the conversation.

3. Analyze the communication and conversation; decide if there was something you could change.

4. Move on and promise to change your faults the next time you may need to speak with the person.

5. Find a way to end the relationship, if at all possible. Again, if kids are involved in a relationship, you will always have to be involved, but you can limit the emotional impact and declutter your mind after each contact. It is a conscious choice.

Emotions

Like relationships, emotions are possible to minimalize. Psychologists are right; talking, reflecting, and depending on you are ways to reduce the negative emotions you carry around. You will come to a time in life when you have more positive emotions. It will require shedding the negative emotions. Personal emotions are harder to alleviate. You have hurt that may be years in the making. But, it is possible to declutter your emotions.

Work Life

Personal emotions should stay out of the workplace, as much as possible. To a point, co-workers are willing to listen to your trouble and to reveal a bit of theirs. However, it is not an everyday desire, nor should it be. At work, you should be there to do a job.

What makes work life emotions difficult is being hurt. You can feel undervalued. You may have issues with a co-worker. Your co-worker may be the one that brings their stuff to work, and it affects their attitude. The good news is that there is a solution. If you keep your life private, your co-worker will stop coming to you. If you keep rebuffing them because work needs to be done, they will no longer stop by.

Beyond the emotional entanglements at work, whether they are hurt feelings by not being recognized for your talents or too much personal stuff being brought to work, you have the space you work in. Decluttering at work allows you to leave your worries at the door, keep your environment clean, and be on hand for all tasks.

It is true that sometimes work and life intersects; you can do your best to reduce these times. You have the power to minimalize work affecting life, and vice versa.

You can also ensure that your workspace is kept clean. Leave the personal items at home or limit yourself to just one photo of the family. Tidy up when you leave each night. There are plenty of other tips, but for now, just remember that decluttering is all about the art of keeping your spaces tidy.

Like your home, you need to declutter your workspace. We all have different places we work, whether we have an office space, vehicle, or little area that becomes cluttered. You also have to work on the emotions that may clutter your work life when they should not.

Your Space

1. Categorize your office.

2. You will have personal items you keep forgetting to take home.

3. You will have items you want there, like pictures, but one will do.

4. Have a place for everything. If your filing cabinet is too small, then see what needs to be moved to make room for the new year. Typically, in an office you remove the current year at the end of that year or beginning of the new year, box up the old, and store the old stuff in a proper location.

5. Get more storage and desk organizers if you need to for decluttering. You should have an in/out box and in progress box to ensure that your desk is always paper free at the end of the day.

For those who do not have an office but rather a vehicle they work in and travel in all day, take your trash out at the end. Keep your items in a bag. Pick up after you eat lunch. Have the company pay for cleaning the inside and outside so the dirt is removed. Dirt can make you feel cluttered. You should not have to feel this.

If you do not have space, then you need to make it a habit of taking all your items home each day or at the end of your workweek. You should not make others view your workplace as messy because you cannot take things home. Yes, you might store coffee in the community kitchen. You might keep veggie dip and veggies in the fridge all week, but when your shifts are over, and you have at least a day in between working, take everything with you. It is both courtesy and minimalism. No one should have to look at your mess, especially when you all have to use that community space.

The work emotions can be hard. You want to share some of your life with people you work with because you consider them friends. However, you should not spend hours discussing personal things. On a good day, spend five minutes. When you have something tough in your life, spend fifteen. Make it clear you want to keep things out of work as much as you can. The best thing you can do is pause at the door of your workplace. Before you turn that handle, say, "I am going to clock in, and that means no more personal thoughts. If I am asked, I will say the minimum to appear nice and not rude."

It does help. It is simple but effective. You can always ask co-workers how they are, but also give guidelines while you ask. "Hey, how are you and the family? I want to know, but give me the short version as I have a million things to do." You can also ask as the person is leaving work or when both of you leave work. There are ways to separate work from personal, and you will be respected for it by the right people. If someone is upset that you no longer seem to care, make it known you are trying to turn over a new life and you still care but want to do so outside of work.

Office

Your office may be a part of your home. It may be a place you can escape that is separate from your home, such as a secondary building on your property. Like work offices, you need to categorize the clutter, cut it down, and then organize it to avoid getting piles of paperwork.

1. Always trash the junk mail before bringing it into your home. Most of us with garages have trashcans near our car. Go through the mail, trash what you need to, and then bring in the bills and other items to your office.

2. Have an incoming pile.

3. Have an outgoing mail section or bills to be paid.

4. When you pay a bill, file it.

5. When you look through something and are done, deem it trash or file it.

6. After you work in your office, take five minutes to clean up, remove the trash to the garage or large trash bin, and leave a clean space.

7. Take thirty minutes a week to dust and vacuum/sweep.

8. Minimize the personal items. This is a workspace, even if it is personal work like taxes, financial reconciliations, and household lists of repair and maintenance. Personal items do not belong.

Life in General

You can declutter your entire life from relationships to work.

1. Create a list.

2. Decide what is useful.

3. Trash what you do not want to keep.

4. Donate what is worthwhile to others but not to you.

5. Find ways to organize what you want.

The golden rule now that you understand minimalism and how to declutter is that for every new item I consider buying and bringing home, one old item must leave. If you are not willing to give up something else, then you cannot bring a new item home.

Also, think about the benefits. How much time you saved, the space you gained, and the option of downsizing to get rid of the costs and space you did not need. These are all factors that will help you declutter your life.

As you work through the relationships section, perhaps even getting rid of the job that does not appreciate you as it should, you are going to find your stress is less and you are happier. The goal is to be happier.

Rules for Decluttering

Why Or How?

It is important to declutter. You probably know how to declutter but knowing the reason makes it easier to declutter. Why do you want to declutter? Why do you need to make space, and what is making some space?

Less isn't the same as nothing.

There is no rule that says that you must get rid of everything. You need to decide what you want in your life. Keep all those things that add some value to your life and learn to enjoy life. When something doesn't add any value to your life, you need to let it go.

It Is Not a Race

Some people find it quite easy to declutter, whereas others take a while longer. You need to remember that you aren't competing with anyone. You must opt for a sustainable pace so that you can stick to it. If someone can de-clutter their home overnight, it doesn't mean that you need to do the same as well. It is better to be consistent instead of worrying about the speed and time taken.

Progress

Progress is progress, regardless of how big or small it is. Even if you take baby steps, it still counts.

Holding On

It might feel difficult to let go, but you don't realize that holding on is even harder. You need to hold on every day. You need to hold on to the things that matter to you. If something doesn't matter to you, then it is better to let go of it. It is much simpler to let go.

Toxic Things to Avoid

Do you know the feeling when you are driving to someplace new and the music in the car is quite loud and at the same time you are trying to understand the directions on the GPS? Then you reach a point on the route that is quite confusing, so you lower the music even though it has no relation to you being lost? Well, that is your life. The volume of the music that you need to decrease to concentrate better? Well, it is all the things that are going on in your life. Once in a while, you do need to lower the volume of the music to concentrate better. This is exactly what decluttering is all about. Decluttering helps you concentrate on the things that matter. Instead of wasting precious time, energy, and resources on tasks, people, and things that don't matter, it does make sense to use them on things that do matter.

In this section, you will learn about certain toxic things that you need to stop doing to live a better life.

Don't take too much notice of what others think. If you want to do something, then go ahead and do it. Don't waste your time thinking about what others might think. Everyone is entitled to their opinion. It is okay to ask for advice. However, you don't always need to worry about the opinions of all those around you. If you want to do something that makes you happy or matters to you, then by all means do it!

Learn to live in the moment. Don't worry about the things that happened in your past or will happen in your future. Don't hold on to all these unnecessary things and instead concentrate on living your life in the moment.

Always surround yourself with people that make you happy. The company that you keep can have a great impact on your life. You will feel happy if you surround yourself with happy people. So, make sure that you surround yourself with people who radiate positive energy. You need to declutter your physical and emotional life as well. Get rid of toxic people from your life.

You cannot feel happy if you are surrounded by cynical and pessimistic people all the time—can you? If you feel that someone is a negative influence in your life, then all that you need to do is let go of that person. It might feel a little difficult initially, but it is better to exclude certain people.

If something makes you miserable, then don't do it. Think about the reasons for why you are doing something. If you cannot find anything positive about it, then it is better to stop doing it.

Don't hold on to any grudges or anger. Holding on to grudges and anger will drain you of your energy. Do you know that the only person who will suffer from holding on to grudges and anger is you? Well, why do you want to hurt yourself unnecessarily? If you can rectify or solve the problem that made you angry, then do so. If you cannot do anything about it, then let go of all the anger. Why do you need to waste your time on something that doesn't hurt anyone else except you?

Learn to resolve issues as soon as possible. It is easier to declutter emotional baggage when you can resolve any issues that you have. If you cannot resolve something or when something is beyond your control, then learn to let go.

You need to stop living in the past. Whatever happened must stay in the past and must not control your life now. You need to learn to let go of your past. Learn from any of your past experiences and use that experience to mold your life at present. Holding on to the past is also a form of clutter that you need to immediately get rid of from your life. How can you ever live life to the fullest if you keep living in the past? Well, take a moment and let that sink in.

Chapter 6

A Tidy Home

Why? It is a question to answer before you consider tidying up your home. Why should you go through all that work? What is the benefit in it for you? We have looked at what it means to live a minimalist lifestyle, what the art of decluttering is all about, and now you need to answer why.

There are several key reasons for keeping your home tidy, but perhaps top two are:

1. Physical health

2. Mental health

Why do you think new teachers catch more colds than teachers who have been in the business longer? Is it that there are more diseases than ten years ago? No, it has nothing to do with the prevalence of diseases. It has nothing to do with better skills in making sure their kids wash their hands and cover their mouth when they cough or sneeze. It has everything to do with exposure to germs. Over time, a teacher gains immunity to certain illnesses like the common cold. They also learn that bringing lunch is a good thing and leaving work at work is healthier than bringing stress home. The point is that each category has distinctive elements that need to be examined so that you can understand the benefit.

Physical Health

Your physical health includes fitness, diseases, and allergies. Removing clutter can ensure you are physically healthier than if you leave the clutter. Why? When you declutter, there are fewer things for dust particles and pet dandruff to settle on. You can also fully clean the surface of your furniture without having to move piles of papers and books. Removing dust and toxins inside your home will cut down on the potential of allergies, diseases, and give you exercise. Cleaning is exercise. You do not need a rowing machine or treadmill to get a workout at home. You just need to have an hour of cleaning.

With decluttering and organizing, you can clean more quickly and more often. It is no longer a horrible job but one that gets done, and then you reap the reward.

Mental Health

Do you have thoughts like, "Oh man, I need to go home and clean" or "I can't stand the mess, but I don't know where to begin"? If you have these thoughts, then you are stressing yourself out. The clutter you see around you and try to cover up shows that you are not attacking the stress, guilt, worry, or fear that is plaguing you. Clutter can also be embarrassing, can cause despair, and add to the family stress. You see a problem but are unable to tackle it because you feel it is too much. When you begin your journey to declutter, you are gaining ground. You start to think positive thoughts because you can see an accomplishment. Suddenly, you are not staring at the piles of paperwork and junk mail but clean surfaces. You have also thrown things away that you didn't need. Your confidence level will increase, as your stress decreases, because of decluttering your home.

More Benefits

There are other benefits to tidying up your home. When you live in a tidy home, you gain so much; it is impossible not to want to get going. Even writing this information makes me, the author, want to stand up, get started, and live a better life, and these practices have already been completed. There is something so worthy and happy about taking charge, decluttering, and becoming a minimalist that it is imperative to share it with you. You can even think of benefits that are not listed based on your personal life. Whatever it will take for you to start decluttering is what you should do after you read through the benefits and various chapters.

- Increased space for more organization and less clutter.

- More time, which you need for family, yourself, and others.

- Happiness when you can go home and relax, without worrying about what you have not done for the day, such as cleaning.

- Calm and peace go hand in hand with decluttering. You do not have to adopt the concept of Zen Buddhism, but often you start to get some of the points—less is more because your worries, stress, and negative emotions are gone. You can go home and meditate in peace, and that is what home should be. Home should be a sanctuary from the rest of the world, but it cannot be if you do not keep it decluttered.

- Passions, hobbies, or whatever you want to call them become possible. You can either go back to enjoying something you have always loved or you can take up a new passion because you have more time, less stress, and tidiness in your home.

You do not need to be a neat freak or an organizing demon to declutter and live like a minimalist, but you are going to lead a tidy, organized life that suddenly feels warm and fuzzy. These are just the whys, and maybe not all of them fit your lifestyle. Perhaps they do. The important takeaway is that you want to strive for a healthier life, where you gain more both physically and mentally.

Five Key Principles

There are five key principles to decluttering your house that are important:

1. A sprint, not a marathon

2. Less is more

3. Breaking the habit of 'just in case'

4. Categories are key

5. The use of space

The five principles listed above will each be explored in their own chapter, with the why and how to help you get started on your journey to declutter and adopt the minimalist mindset. It is best to start with one principle and fully understand it before you move on to the next. Some chapters may have more information than others because of the in-depth tips and strategies being provided. Other chapters will be more about the why versus the how. In the end, you are going to better understand what it means to have a tidy home, especially now that you know the benefits.

Get ready, take notes if you wish, and start getting your plan ready to declutter, organize, and live the minimalist lifestyle.

Chapter 7

A Sprint, Not a Marathon

Are you a sprinter or a marathon runner? Marathon runners build up to a long race. Conditioning helps set a consistent pace, one that they continue throughout the race. Sprinters do a short run, and then it is over. There are benefits to being both types of runners when it comes to the concept of decluttering. Disadvantages also exist for both.

A declutter marathon is never-ending. You start small, and by the time the entire house is clutter free, you have to go back through it. Sometimes a person never finishes. It can seem like a time-saver, spending ten minutes to remove clutter. For the right person, it is. If your priorities are on your family, seven years to declutter is not unreasonable.

Another benefit of the marathon is lower stress. Sometimes when there is an overwhelming project, our minds lose focus or stop altogether. We spend more time planning where to begin rather than starting.

Often this type of person has so much going on in their life that large projects may cause anxiety, fear, and stress. If you know your psychology fits this description, consider going for a short marathon. Begin in the main room and declutter. Testing yourself will help you decide whether or not to become a sprinter.

A sprinter sees the large project and carves out the time to complete it. The downside is how tiring such a sprint is because you are going to ache. The pain can equal the reward at the end though, such as a soak in a hot tub.

The benefits of being a sprinter add up to more than a marathon mindset. Yes, marathon runners feel less stress. They begin work on their home and do so each weekend or a little at the end of each day. However, if you go for the entire cleanup all at once, you can clean your entire home once or twice a year. You declutter and remain tidy, so you are never stressed about how much is left to do.

Benefits of Being a Sprinter

- You do not have to declutter every weekend, once you have a system in place.

- Doing a major clean once or twice a year allows you to have more free time for the things you love.

- Getting it all done at once gets every nook and cranny clean—you avoid cleaning the same areas over and over again by decluttering everything at the same time.

- You no longer focus on what must be done because it is all complete.

- You give yourself less time to quibble over sentimental items.

- You take three or four days to get the work done, and then it is over; you put a system in place, and then you don't think about the mess. You always walk into a clean home, with just vacuuming, dusting, and mopping required.

- You can get back to that hobby.

- You can fulfill a promise you make to someone.

- You have more time for family and friends.

- You can read a book.

- You can write a book.

- You can do a project, such as a home improvement you wanted to do but never had time for.

The benefits of being a sprinter can go on and on. The question is what value do you gain from decluttering all at once, instead of slowly over time? The answers are above.

Psychological Interference

It is hard sometimes to think about the task before us. We want certain things in life, and suddenly we are unable to obtain them or our wants change. Minimalists have a mindset change. Their psychology adopts a less is more concept, where the material item is not as important.

Perhaps one of the greatest movies of the last decade was "The Confessions of a Shopaholic?", mentioned earlier. It is a shopaholic who maxed out her credit cards and could no longer afford her lifestyle. She had to start selling things to pay her debts. Challenges are going to arise, but the quicker you move through the decluttering work and start organizing, the quicker you are going to see the benefits. It is like the hot tub example for the sprinter. Yes, you might spend two days going through a house, trashing things, donating items, and keeping what you want with more organization, but at the end of those two days, you can reward your work.

There is nothing to say that you cannot reward yourself for the steps you take. In fact, it is encouraged. You just have to know how to get around that mind-blocking phase when a large project is too much.

Let's consider a garage cleanup. Everywhere you look is stuff. So much stuff, you cannot park your car in that garage. You cannot think of how to start, much less find reward for doing so, until you change your psychology and go for the sprint.

1. Get the trash in one area.

2. Remember, you get to park in the garage when you are done.

3. Anything that is going to be donated goes into your car, now!

4. If you are going to sell items, post them while you soak in the hot tub.

When you look at a decluttering job like the garage, as written in the four steps, it becomes more doable, right? You have a plan, you have organization, and you have a goal. Sprinters have goals. They just like to have those goals met in a short time to reap the numerous benefits. Keep the sprinter benefits in mind, set a plan, and think only of the section of the plan you are on as you work through your sprint. You will no longer feel a marathon is required once you take those tips to heart.

Chapter 8
Less Is More

Throughout the chapters of this book thus far, we have explored the minimalist mindset, how to transition, and the concept of decluttering. These principles still apply to less is more. The minimalists have realized that more things do not make them happy. It does not give them time to enjoy what they own. Ask yourself—how many movies can you watch at one time? Yes, the answer is one. So, why do you need 500 DVDs if you can only watch one movie at a time? Even a person with thirty DVDs gets tired of watching the same thing. In one month, all thirty movies can be seen, and will a repeat occur the next month? Probably not. The digital age helps us keep less but have access to more.

If you need to, take a moment to write out your minimalist goals. What do you hope to gain or benefit from a tidy home as you take on the less is more concept? Seeing these goals in your handwriting can be extremely beneficial to you. It can also keep them present in your mind as you begin working on decluttering with an aim toward minimalizing your life.

When decluttering your house, you are going to consider two things:

1. Getting rid of everything you do not love or need

2. Organizing what you do love and need

Decluttering without Sentimentality

Are you already balking at what you have to get rid of? You might be looking around and saying, "Man, I have a lot of stuff." These are typical reactions. Everyone goes through them. There are a series of questions you can ask to help you declutter your home and own less. For everything, if you are not able to put in the trash, donate, or sell pile right away, ask the questions.

Organizing Your Decluttering Process

- Get at least three trash bags, bins, or boxes.

- Use four sticky notes—write trash, donate, sell, keep.

- Put those notes in four separate areas of the room you are starting with.

- Use more sticky notes if you have large items that cannot be moved.

The Questions

1. Have you used that item in the last six to twelve months?

2. What sentimental value does it have?

3. Do I love it?

4. Is there a place to store it?

5. How often will I need to dust it or the area it belongs to?

Examples are helpful for working through your hesitancy to get rid of items. So, here are steps with examples.

1. You pull a pair of pants out of the closet.

2. You have not worn these pants in a year.

3. You try them on.

4. They do not fit.

5. There are no holes, no fading of the color, and they are in decent shape.

6. The pants go in the donation bin.

Right there, you have gotten rid of one item. You are letting it go to a home that will use it.

1. You pull out a picture.

2. It is a picture you have not looked at in over a year.

3. This picture has two friends who died in it.

4. It is the only picture with one of those friends.

5. You will keep it.

6. You will upload it on to your computer and save it in the Cloud. Perhaps you will make a background image of it on your home screen.

In this example, you have something that is sentimental, but taking up space. You do not want to lose sight of the picture because every year or two it is nice to go back and see these friends who died too young. You have lessons you learned from them or good stories you tell because of them. However, keeping the print is not necessary.

From both examples, you should have a way to start tackling the sentimental and non-sentimental decluttering steps that you need to do. A book cannot tell you if you should get rid of something or adapt how you keep it. The idea is to gain some knowledge from the tips and try to move on to the next pile.

When you declutter with the strategy less is more, you should take no longer than a minute to decide on most items.

You should never set something aside to "determine" later. As you work through each room, it is time to decide if it will stay or go. The longer you give to the reflection of what the item could mean, the more difficult it is to get rid of it.

Changing to a minimalist mindset is about changing how you think and breaking the cycle you have been in during your life.

86

The Inheritance

Will someone enjoy what you have to pass on or send it to the dump? Here is a new way of looking at it.

1. You get your family to your home.

2. You have your family help you with the pile you created of inheritance items.

3. You let your family pick what they want.

4. They take it home.

5. Ah, the minimalist in you is satisfied.

The benefit of "now" is that your family gets to enjoy the item and you no longer have to deal with it. Maybe in two years they decide they do not want it and pass it to another family member. Perhaps they get rid of it completely. Your choice was made. It left, and you decluttered your home, with the concept that less is more.

You can do this with china, furniture, clothing, baby clothing, baby books, tax records, and a host of other things you might be storing. There is never a need to keep anything in your home if you think it has a place to go or unless you want to have it until you die.

You can do the same with pictures. You upload them, send them on, or get rid of them. If you are old enough to have children, nieces, nephews, or other family that will want to take some of the things that you no longer use or want in your home, follow through with the inheritance concept.

One person who decluttered a bunch of her spouse's items after he passed away, loaded up her car, drove to her kids' homes, and left the boxes there. Now they had to go through them and decide what to keep or trash.

Do not think you are in this alone, when you have family grown or not. In fact, a great lesson you can provide your young children, if you have any, is that less is more.

Show your child that they do not have to keep a toy they played with five years ago as a two-year-old. Remove the toys, games, and books that are not used by helping your child understand that an unused item can be given to someone else. It can bring joy to another.

When you are done with something or no longer use something, you can pass it on. Children learn from examples. If you do not keep a shirt with holes in it because it is a favorite, your child is more apt to get rid of their shirt.

The lesson that less is more is valuable, and it starts at a young age, as well as sharing, giving to those in need, and learning that doing is better than shopping and spending.

When you are done with this step, move on to breaking some other bad habits.

Declutter

You should have a plan for how you are going to tackle your home and make sure you have less so you can do more. Keep this plan handy and learn about breaking those habits that might interfere with your new mindset.

Chapter 9

Breaking the Habit of *'Just in Case'*

We all tend to have a lot of 'just in case' items lying around the house. Well, the 'just in case' way of thinking can extend to all aspects of your life. If you want to declutter, then you need to let go of all the things that you don't need and the things that don't add any value to your life. It also means that you need to learn to let go of all the just in case items.

The just in case kind of thinking can lead to accumulation of items that you will probably never use. For instance, you probably have a couple of items of clothing in your wardrobe that you will never wear, but you still hold on to them. It can be a pair of skinny jeans that no longer fit you. You probably hold on to it in the hope that one day it will fit you again. Or maybe you own a blouse that you know you will never wear, but it is still kept safely in the cupboard. So, why do you hold on to such things? After all, they are just things and you cannot possibly hurt their feelings if you discard them. There is a fine line between holding on to things in the name of wishful thinking and hoarding.

You need to discard all the things that you don't use. A simple rule that you can use to address this issue is the 20/20 rule. This rule is quite simple. If you can replace an item for $20 and within 20 minutes, then you don't need to hold on to it just in case. If something is easily replaceable, then you don't need it.

For instance, a newly married couple moves into their new house. They start to purchase all the necessary utensils and silverware that they will need to entertain any guests. They do entertain guests from time to time. It excites them whenever they have guests over. It also excites the couple whenever they use any of the utensils or silverware. So, every time they go out shopping, they buy more and more, always thinking that it's just in case more friends come over. As the years pass, their once beautiful house starts filling up with stuff, stuff they do not even need as often. Accumulating or keeping stuff just in case is never a good habit.

Well, it is quite easy to replace kitchen utensils, and it hardly takes any time to replace them. So, if you have five sets of dinner plates, then maybe you can keep two sets and discard the rest.

You might think that it is quite wasteful to get rid of items or all such things that fall under the just in case category. However, take a moment and think about it. Isn't it better to get rid of things and declutter your home and life, instead of holding on to things that you probably will never use?

Most of us have the bad habit of keeping things just in case. You think that you will keep the items in the event you need them, so your home begins to pile up with things. You think, "Sometimes I use this" or "Every two years I needed this." These thoughts ensure you keep more than you need and certainly more than you want to have sitting around your home.

You need to let go. You need to ask a question:

Will I ever use it? If so, when?

If you cannot come up with a concrete answer shortly, then you need to get rid of it.

Let's go back to the clothing example. You have a beautiful suit. You are ten pounds heavier than to be able to wear it. You have been this way for six years. Each year, you keep saying you will lose enough weight to wear it again, but that never happens. Now you think, "Ah, but I am adopting minimalism, so I will get out and do more things, which will lead to a healthier life and less weight." Gotcha. You fell into the trap. Yes, you have the potential to lose weight to fit that item, and more so if you lead a healthier life due to your new minimalist mindset, but you should not keep the item.

You are "hoping" for change. You might even see the item as a reward for that change, but in six years—it has not been enough—you are still in the place you were, and you cannot use that item.

Just like any item that is a year old, you need to get rid of things you "hope" will be useful. Consider for a moment the survivalist type. Survivalists tend to stockpile certain canned goods. They think they must have ten or more of something in case the world goes wrong, in the event they need to live in a bunker, but look what happens. Every few years, something they keep meets its expiration date.

The just in case habit you have should be viewed as an expiration date. Has the item reached the end of its life? Would it kill you if you eat it? The idea is thinking in this manner will help you get rid of an item, whether it is clothes, books, or food.

Keeping something around that has no use to you and will not have a use, except perhaps once in a blue moon, is costing you space and time.

Here are a couple of questions that you can ask yourself whenever you start to declutter.

- Do I really need this?
- Will I ever use this?
- Do I even like using it?
- Why do I want to hold on to it?
- Does it have any sentimental value for me?
- If I do keep it, then how often will I use it?
- Will I be able to live without it?
- Can I replace it if I ever need it?
- Will I spend money to buy something like this again?

- What purpose does it serve?
- Does it make me happy?
- What can I do with the space that I save?

Take a moment and answer these questions truthfully. You will have the answer to your problem.

Saving Space

The kitchen is always a great place to go when thinking about just in case situations. People who live in the mountains are told to have water on hand, food in cans, and enough supplies for at least a week or two. Okay, great, but what happens if a blizzard never comes—do you keep storing it?

No. If you are a wise person living in the mountains, you stockpile for the winter and save space in the summer. You are going to first eat all the perishable items that will expire and then attack the canned goods that expire, and throughout the summer you eat what you have. You shop less but also buy more fresh items. Just before winter comes, you start to store up things you can eat if the power goes out and you are without heat and water for a few days or weeks.

The cycle ensures you never have the just in case problem. You never see your items expire before you can eat them.

It does not have to be only food, but it is the best example. Saving space throughout your home is possible when you do not keep anything just in case. For instance, the taxman wants you to keep files for seven years if you run a business. You could be audited for up to seven years. But, we are in the digital age. Do you need those big boxes, or can you have your files digitally stored? The chances of you needing your tax documents from seven years ago are limited, so a digital file is acceptable.

Have you looked at your paper files recently? Paper is different than decades ago when the rule of seven was put in place. Your receipts that the IRS may want fade. The date, amount spent, and other things disappear, and it doesn't take a year to make that happen. In a few weeks, you can see the ink coming off a receipt depending on where it is stored and how it is stored. Saving digital copies due to ink and paper problems is not only a space saver but smart.

You do not have to be in the just in case mind mode because there are better ways of keeping certain things. There are better habits to have. Not everything is possible to eliminate when it comes to specific circumstances, but in general, you can find a way to reduce the clutter and save space.

1. What is the item?

2. Why was it kept?

3. Is the reason for keeping it gone?

4. Do you have a use for it? Is it an applicable use or a 'hope to use'?

5. What can you do with the space if the item goes?

6. Are the benefits of tidying up weighing more heavily than keeping the item?

If you answer these questions and find you still have a solid reason to keep something, okay, but more often than not, you will discover there are many reasons why you should not keep your habit of just in case.

Time Saving 101

You already know that time is gained when you declutter. We examined the timing of cleaning a house with and without the clutter. You know you can save time on cleaning once a week by hitting the important areas, which are no longer cluttered, and by doing a deep clean once or twice a year.

Now, imagine if you stopped putting things in the wrong place. What if you came home, had a place for the mail, and you did not have to declutter every few days? You would save time.

You are going to see a chapter later on the use of space, which will delve more into what happens when you organize your life for the benefit of using the space you have better. For now, concentrate on the fact that you can have more space and time when you decide to break the habit of just in case. You do not have to clean as often.

Another benefit of solving the just in case shopping issue, such as stocking up on various food items to prevent starvation, is time. You are not shopping to fill the space because you broke the habit of buying things you do not need just in case you might one day want it or use it.

You can save time with a variety of things in this way. You are looking to keep the essentials in your home. This allows you to have only what you are going to use, or currently use, versus what you will never actually need.

Part of the timesaving portion of breaking your habits is to reduce your "need" in the stores. You will want to think through what you write on the shopping list.

Let's use an example. You decide you are going to a store for coffee. You do not get to this store often because it is out of the way. There is not one in your town but one forty minutes away. You will stock up because, in three months, you will be out of this coffee. You walk in and see a plethora of items. You start looking for fun and then your just in case mind steps in. It says, "Oh, wouldn't that be lovely sitting on the mantle" or "I can use that every other time I have tea," and before you know it, you buy something you do not need.

Going to the shop with a list of what you are going to buy will eliminate the just in case habit you have. You are going to save time because you are not going to wander around and think about what you could buy or might need. Instead, you go in for the one item, put blinders on, and walk out with only what you went in for.

Instead of spending forty minutes in a store, you spent ten. So, the moral of this example is to create a list, enter, and leave, always with the mindset that you only need what you wrote down and nothing else.

Saving time is not just about the decluttering but the mindset you are gaining as you declutter and consider what is useful and not in the event that something occurs. Yes, it is possible to buy fifty safety pins, but do you need that many? Do you have a place to store them? If you only need one because your button broke, then buy the minimal amount. So, just remember breaking your habits is about reducing clutter, getting rid of items you do not need, and preventing yourself from buying more.

A Few Last Tips

1. You do not have to be wasteful.

2. You can donate your items of use to someone else.

3. You can also sell certain things that are in demand.

4. Think of ways to benefit from what you are decluttering.

5. Consider looking outside the box.

6. Ask yourself, what would a realtor, a friend, or family member think if they saw your home or the item you are hesitating about?

Embarrassment can be a helpful emotion. It is not always helpful as it is also a mental health issue when you get too stressed about the situation; however, when it comes to decluttering and making that sacrifice to get rid of something, embarrassment can be helpful. You suddenly realize that you do not need the item and want to break the cycle. For others, the emotional crutch can be a different emotion. You might like the satisfaction of the accomplishment that allowed you to get rid of an item for good. Whatever it takes, use those emotions to move on with your life and become a minimalist.

Chapter 10

Categories Are Key

You can take another chunk of decluttering fear away by adding categories to your process. Some people like to do a room-by-room cleaning while others feel better gathering all like items in one place. Either way can work, and you can decide which method you think fits your lifestyle.

Bedroom Example

Room-by-room means you start in the bedroom, organize it, and then move on. It's best to empty out your closet to get started so that when you tackle the rest of your bedroom you have a place to put some of the items you want to stash out of sight. A good rule of thumb is if you haven't worn it in a year, get rid of it. Space is precious, and it should only be occupied by clothing that makes you feel and look good. That favorite t-shirt that is stained and so tattered that it makes you look like you have been living on a deserted island for years needs to find a place in the trash bin.

There should be at least three bins, boxes, or trash bags in residence before you begin. A flat surface is most helpful, but if you can't get it done in one day, don't clutter up your bed; it's not conducive to sleeping. A chest of drawers could work or. as a last resort. the floor. Now that you have all your clothes, shoes, jewelry, and miscellaneous merchandise removed from your closet, clean it. Starting fresh and clean will give you more incentive to complete your mission.

Do you need five pairs of tennis shoes? Six pairs of black shoes or a shoe in every color? If you wear them on a regular basis for work or because it is who you are, then find a way to contain them in your new zone. If not, use your three clutter free sources to downsize.

Once you have your closet in good shape, take a look at your linens. Are they scattered about your bedroom or do you have so many you could open a store? Faded sheets or dry, stiff towels and washcloths need to be dumped. This opens up more space for feel-good linens.

The Categories

As you can tell from the bedroom example, there are always those questions of what to get rid of, what you want to keep, and what you need to organize. You are going to learn a bit more about the use of space as you continue on your journey through this book. For now, the focus is on why going category-by-category rather than room-by-room may be helpful.

Who does not have shoes in at least two different places? I do not know of one person who has all their shoes in one closet. Most women tend to have dress shoes in the bedroom and daily shoes in a closet near the door or on the floor by the main exit. So, what if you had categories, where you gather up every same item, go through it, and get rid of what is no longer worth keeping? You might find it is a little easier than going room by room to get through the clutter. There are many examples of different categories:

1. Shoes

2. Clothes

3. Pictures (digital and prints)

4. Utensils

5. Linens

6. Books

7. Magazines

8. Notebooks

9. Paperwork

10. Office items

You can make your own categories; however, the ones supplied here give you an idea of what it means to go room-by-room or category-by-category. For example, let's say you are looking at linens. If you have three bedrooms that are lived in, two bathrooms, and a kitchen, you probably have linens for all three rooms, towels in the bathrooms, and kitchen towels. Gather them up in one space, go through them, and put away only what you will keep based on the quality and usefulness they offer.

You will do this with each category. Once one category is done, you move on. You get to check it off the list. It can be exciting to go with categories because you know you have made headway on a specific group of items versus going through more towels, linens, or shoes later on.

It is not a concept that works for everyone, but you may find it is the best choice for you. Some people like the room-by-room method because then one large chunk of the house is done, and they do not have to run from room to room to make sure they have everything that fits the category. You could also go room to room, targeting that one specific category, creating a pile of trash as you move and storing what you keep as you eliminate other things.

Do what works for you.

Chapter 11

Use of Space

Congratulations, you have decluttered and now have a new palette for your remaining household goods and more closet space. What you do now could keep you organized or send you right back into the same clutter trap. Staying on the road to organization is easier than you might think. There are so many ways to enjoy a peaceful co-existence with your belongings.

You will discover some helpful tips for each room of the house in this chapter. You may need a couple of things to get started depending on what you already have in your home. Of course, if you are like most people out there, you may not need a thing because you already have storage bins and organizers—they were just too full until you decluttered.

You might think that organization is a part of the decluttering process, but actually, it is far better if you declutter first and then start to look toward an organizational system. The reason for this is that you may continue to declutter and never finish. You might be always trying to declutter and organize at once, but without finishing one or the other. You have learned about decluttering by category, as well as organizing by category. What you want to remember from what you read throughout the book and also in this section is that you learn first, plan, and then implement.

The use of space concept is to help you keep in mind what you may have to store as you work through decluttering by category. If you know how many pairs of shoes you need to store once you declutter, you can then organize them. If you have dress shoes and daily use shoes, you are apt to keep these two things separate due to space limitations. These are just a few of the things to think about as you work through this chapter.

The Bedroom

Let's begin with your bedroom, as this is where you want to have a calm environment for not only sleeping but unwinding from the daily activities of your life. You could hire a closet organizer and spend a good deal of money, or you can take the do-it-yourself approach and reap monetary benefits and confidence building skills in the process. A planner that lists all that needs to go into your closet is a good place to start. Think of putting all your blouses, shirts, jackets, and sweaters in the same area. Pants, trousers, and anything else you have with legs can go next. Skirts and long dresses can go to the sides of the closet; longer clothing articles aren't used as much and so can be relegated to a more remote area in the closet.

Now that you have a plan for the sections of clothing, let's talk about using the rainbow for further organization. Think ROYGBIVN R for red, O for orange, Y for yellow, G for green, B for blue, I for indigo, V for violet, and N for neutrals. Black and whites can be placed in the front or the back of this color line. Just imagine how getting ready for your day will take less time with this method. Putting together an outfit for work or play is going to be a snap with this technique.

The majority of your clothing is now looking polished and ready for action. If you are one that likes to have shelves in your closet for folded articles such as sweaters, lingerie, and whatever else is not hanger friendly, then baskets or pull out shelves should work for you. Shoe racks or shelves for shoes or hanging cubbies also work well. Organize your shoes by color as you did your clothing.

If you have a dresser that you like or is part of a bedroom set, think about putting it in your closet if there is room. Why? This will leave you with more space in your bedroom for a nice cozy chair or love seat for relaxation. Designing a quiet retreat should be part of your new organization to live clutter free. Think outside the norm when looking for ways to keep knickknacks and other mementos visible without creating chaos. A picture frame or shadow box is a unique way to keep your jewelry handy. A plant stand can be used in your closet for organizing if you don't have shelves. A spinning tie holder is a great way to give your scarves a place to live without taking up a lot of space.

The Bathroom

Bathrooms can be a catchall for all sorts of things that sit on your countertop. It is hard to think of getting ready for your day when you have to move your lotions and makeup to get your toothbrush. If you don't have a medicine chest, then you may be relying on drawers to keep everything tidy. Are you one who just dumps facial creams, cleansers, and other like products in a drawer? Get it together with a simple silverware compartment basket. They come in many interesting forms. A wooden silverware basket adds an elegant element to your drawer. Wire baskets are another great example of keeping your drawers clutter free. I have even seen cupcake and muffin tins up to the challenge. All of these ideas for your organizational needs do not have to cost you a fortune. Dollar stores have quite a selection of solutions for storage containment.

The Kitchen

Let's take a look at your kitchen next, as you will no doubt spend a fair amount of time there. Pot racks, if you have an overhead space, is a great way to open up cupboard space. They are perfect for an island or above or near the stove, depending on the layout of your kitchen. If you don't have room for a pot rack as you have an end cabinet, pick up some plumbing pipe and make a pot holder, which would give an exciting use to an unusual element. Get some hooks, and you are organized.

Lazy Susan's also present a good use of space. They can be used for everyday food storage items such as cereal, coffee, and baking ingredients. You can then put bakeware and items that might be stuck on the countertop out of sight in your cupboards. If you have a pantry, then use baskets or install rollout shelves in this area to give you more usable space. Glass or plastic storage containers inside your cabinets also give a huge thank you to organization. Magazine holders can be a creative way to hold your water bottles.

Linens can go in pretty baskets with labels. This saves time and space, as they tend to fall over if kept on shelves. If you think about it, many items are used in an office that could be put to work in other areas of the home. Corkboard could be added to the back of a cabinet door. You can use this as a place to put a calendar with schedules, keys, or anything that needs its small place. You can also paint the back of a cabinet door with blackboard paint to serve the purpose of informing the family of upcoming events.

The Laundry Room

Laundry areas can be a huge source of clutter because they do a lot of dirty work. If you can install cabinets over your washer and dryer, then you are going to be ahead of the clutter game. If you only have space for a single cabinet, put it in the middle of the area with shelves on each side; it looks more pleasing to the eye and achieves the same effect. Organization is still needed behind closed doors though. Delegate a particular area for like items and again use dividers to keep them in place or the ever present basket. A three-bin laundry basket can corral dirty clothes from the floor. Nothing says clutter like clothes that take on a life of their own on the floor. Remember to put a wastebasket in the laundry room for trash and lint. I have seen macramé plant holders with wicker baskets in them to hold lint and small waste, so if space is a concern you have a solution.

A money saving tip for getting a cabinet for your laundry room is to head to a thrift store or a closeout sale. Can't afford that? Pick up a single piece of nicely finished wood at a home improvement store, then get barn door hardware and make a cabinet door for your shelves. It can hide your soaps and cleaning supplies while the other side of your shelf holds cookbooks or little-used cookware or plants.

The Family Room, Den, and Parlor

The most prominent area to keep in shape is most likely a living room or family room. You may have a space for a desk in this area, and, if you do, use it wisely. Paper clutter is the most difficult to deal with especially if you have a flat surface family. That means if there is a flat surface available your family will leave it there until it turns to dust or is removed. Remove this temptation by giving them something tangible to put all those pieces of paper in. A file cabinet with folders for each member of the household is a great way to stay clutter free. For the critical documents that must be dealt with immediately, get an in-basket so everyone knows to check it regularly. Then, once it has been taken care of, put it in an out-basket for picking up. It's neat and an effective way to make sure that field trip note is signed and returned on time.

Books can be an essential part of a family room, as are games. A couch height shelving unit can be decorative and a great place to store these items. You could get a unit with doors on it to hide the collection or again make some inexpensive doors to compliment your décor. Roll out shelves or other kitchen organization helpers can be purchased to go inside the cabinets. Stackable shelves that dishes can be placed on are excellent sources of space savers. If the shelves are a little deeper, get turntables to make finding things more comfortable.

Toys often are found in a family room and shout clutter louder than anything other than the children. If at all possible, invest in closed-door units to incorporate structure in this area. Baskets inside the unit will keep balls and other objects that can tumble out contained. Another staple from the laundry area is a three-bin hamper. It is a great place to store stuffed animals or sporting equipment.

If you have the space, try to put a small table in a corner area for crafting or homework. When the crafting items are not in use, they can go into your storage area. If you can't fit a storage unit like that in your room, plan on storage baskets that can fit under the table. A cool table that folds down flat against a wall is also a good solution.

Hinge it and make it with folding legs while not in use, and it can be a decorative focal point in your room.

Giving the kids a place for their stuff will keep your living area neater and teach responsibility to your kids as well as good cleaning habits. You might even want to make a room divider with a bookcase or folding screen to further cordon off an area for play. A folding screen room divider with open spaces is a perfect place to put 2x6 pieces of wood to make some shelves for storing small items. Don't rule out finding an old chest of drawers at a thrift shop that can be refurbished to create a super toy chest.

The endless array of cords is another eyesore when you have decluttered. The entertainment area is a place that you see when you are watching television or enjoying a quiet moment reading a book or just relaxing. Who wants to look at a jungle of cords? Zip ties and hooks are your friends in this area. Get some of those hooks that hang on the wall but don't damage the paint. Take your zip ties and roll up the cords to the right height, then hang them on the hooks. While you will most likely still see the cords, they won't be lying on the floor like a pile of entwined snakes.

While we're still in entertainment mode, let's deal with all the remotes that go with your devices. If you're lucky enough to have a single control, good for you. Most people have at least two or more. They make hanging pouches that go over the arm of a sofa or chair, which is convenient but not always aesthetically pleasing. A decorative basket or planter can be a great place to keep these errant devices. It can fit on a shelf, on an end table, or even on the floor. If your end table has a drawer, put them in a silverware container in there. Magazines can be put in a wire half file that stands on end, typically used in an office.

If you have plants in your home, you can put them on tables with a lamp, design a plant stand on your own, or buy one of the many offerings at garden centers. If the plants are small enough, a unique way to display them that takes up a minimum of wall space is to get a decorative candleholder. Succulents are a great plant to use this item for as their small round pots fit ideally in the candleholder.

This should take care of most of the spaces in your home that need organization. If you feel clutter creeping back into your life, take a look at your home through an outsider's eyes. The next time you walk into your home, view it as though it is your first time seeing it. Is it pleasing to you, or do you sense that things are again taking over your space? If it is the latter, don't hesitate to jump on the organization train. You can bring in a new design piece if it goes with your new clutter-free lifestyle, but take one item out. You can always maintain a peaceful, restful home if you follow your new organizational plan.

Chapter 12

New Beginnings Are the Best

It might seem difficult to stay motivated at times. Also, there will be times when you feel like giving up. In this section, you will learn about motivation and the ways in which you can motivate yourself to start afresh.

Motivation is of two types, and you can classify them in any manner that you want to. The most uncomplicated classification is positive and negative motivation. An even simpler classification can be pain and pleasure. Every act that we do, every thought that we have, and every belief that we hold has its foundation in either pain or pleasure. The view of pain and pleasure will vary from one individual to another. The associations that we make toward pain and pleasure are all buried deep in our subconscious, and most people never realize this. Instead of going through life on autopilot, it can helpful if you take a look around and think about why you are doing something instead of just doing it. It isn't difficult to learn and shift the way you perceive a given situation. Something that might seem like a problem to you can be turned into an opportunity with just a little bit of practice.

So, it is safe to say that all motivation is internal motivation. If you believe that there is more pleasure to gain than pain to experience if you do a particular thing, then your motivation for doing that particular act will be greater; if you believe that something will just bring you pain, the chances of you going ahead and doing that are much lower.

If you want to be able to change your motivation and you want to maneuver it in your favor, then you will have to work on reframing your associations. For instance, if you're going to shed a few pounds, but you just aren't motivated to exercise, then here are some assumptions that you might have formed in your mind that are holding you back from doing what you ought to do. You might be of the opinion that exercise has never really worked out for you, that working out in a gym makes you feel bad when you compare yourself to others, and that you don't have enough time for exercising and, even if you did, it really wouldn't make any difference. You probably have the opinion in your mind that you have more fun when you are relaxing and indulging in an activity that you like instead of exercising.

There are steps for reframing the associations that exist in your mind. The first step is to replace the pain with pleasure. The first three assumptions in the above example were all associated with pain, and the last one alone was associated with pleasure, but it wasn't related to the task at hand. It is an obvious deduction that there are more associations with pain than with pleasure, and it means that you will associate exercising with pain and thus be discouraged to exercise. There is an immediate need for reframing those assumptions to try and see the pleasure of exercising instead of pain. Here are some instances that might help. Think along the lines that if exercising can work for others, then it can work for you as well. If you go to a gym, you can see others who have to manage creating an exercise routine; instead of thinking of this as a pain, think of it as being inspiring. Every time you exercise, you are taking a step toward a healthier life, and it will make you feel good. You can always consider taking up some fun exercises and involving yourself in other activities that interest you and will also provide the necessary exercise that your body needs.

The second step is to add some pain to all the pleasure that you have been thinking about. Turning all the pain points associated with exercising into pleasure points will prove to be sufficient motivation for some to get started. But others might need a little more motivation. Think of all the pain that you will experience if you don't exercise. Here are specific examples that will help you get a better understanding. If you will put on weight if you don't exercise, you won't be able to achieve the body that you have always wanted. You won't be able to lead a healthier life since exercising isn't a habit of yours. You won't be a good role model for your family members who look up to you. You can keep going until you have managed to inspire and motivate yourself to work harder. The associations that you have can be a really strong influence in determining whether or not you have the motivation for achieving the things that you want.

You will need to get out of your comfort zone if you want to do something new. You will need to motivate yourself to step out of the shell that you have created for yourself if you want to embrace change and try something different. People tend to get comfortable with the way things are, and they stop trying to look for new ways that they can challenge themselves for their development. We tend to become complacent with the way things are with our lives and all those things that seem to affect us. You will need to realize that you have the power and the choice of making any changes that you want to make, and you can start taking control of your own life. But all this requires a lot of self-motivation, and you can make use of all these techniques for taking charge of your life by staying motivated and also by keeping control of the positive motivation that is much required. You will have to take that one step and step out of your comfort zone if you want to do great things and have experiences that make you feel satisfied.

Steps to Stay Motivated

Define what you want to accomplish. You cannot achieve anything if you don't have an objective in mind. Your goal can be to declutter your life, start afresh, or anything else. If you want to start afresh, then there are certain things that you need to do. You need to be able to let go of all the things that don't add any value to your life. If you feel that something is holding you back, then it is time to let go of it.

Make a note of your reasons for doing so. We all tend to do certain things consciously or subconsciously. However, the move to declutter is a conscious decision, and you need to work hard on it. If you feel like you don't have the necessary motivation to keep going, then make sure that you revisit your reasons for making the changes that you are.

Try to visualize how you will feel when you achieve your goal. Don't just visualize your goal, but also make a note of how you will feel if you don't do it. The idea of pain can also work as motivation.

Set mini goals or small goals that will help you achieve your primary goal. For instance, if you want to declutter your home, then your mini goals can be to declutter the living room in a week, then to declutter the bedroom, kitchen, and so on.

You can always break down your goals into smaller goals. Doing this will help make your goal seem more achievable. Not just that, it will help you measure your progress as well. Setting and accomplishing small goals will provide you with the necessary motivation to keep going.

Regardless of what your goal is about, you need to schedule some time for it. Note it in your calendar, set a reminder, and treat it like any other regular appointment. You will not be able to achieve all your goals if you don't commit. If you feel that you are having some trouble sticking to the schedule, then think about all the reasons for which you are doing it.

Create a checklist of all the mini goals you have established for yourself. Doing this will help you keep track of your progress. If you feel that you are lagging somewhere, you can put in some extra effort to improve your performance and progress.

It is very likely that you will run into some hurdles during your journey toward success. So, you need to have a plan to overcome all those hurdles. Take some time and think about all the likely obstacles you will come across. Once you know this, you can think of solutions or alternative routes that you can make use of. If you do this, you won't feel unmotivated whenever you come across an obstacle. Instead, you will have a plan that will keep you going.

You must always maintain a positive attitude. You can use positive affirmations to make yourself feel good about your goal. Positive self-talk is also quite beneficial.

Tips to Live a Stress-Free Life

Commitment

Regardless of the goals you have in life, you need to commit to those goals if you want to accomplish them. A commitment will help you to take the necessary steps to make the constant improvements to achieve your goals. Without commitment, the goals will just be ideas. It can be anything; you might want to launch a startup, lose weight, or even just take a cooking class. Whatever your goal is, you need commitment. Commitment provides you with the motivation to keep going.

People Care about You

Let me be very honest now. Those who matter to you and to whom you matter, they care about you. They don't care about the clothes you wear, the car you drive, your bank balance, or the house you live in. It doesn't mean that they don't respect your progress or achievements. There is more to life than just the superficial things that we all concentrate on. These people care about you, and they will support you because they love you. Remember that you are loved, even when you cannot like yourself.

Learn to Be Grateful

You need to be thankful for all the good that happens to you. If you aren't grateful, you will never fully appreciate anything in life.

When you are grateful, you will feel better about yourself. So, make it a habit to be thankful for at least one thing daily. When you are thankful, it brings a sense of contentment, and that will make you happy.

Take Action

Confidence and competence go hand in hand. If you want to achieve something in life, you need to take action. Even small steps on a daily basis can make a huge difference in the long run. Your ideas might be brilliant, but they won't amount to anything if you don't act on those ideas.

Money Cannot Buy Happiness

A little retail therapy might help you feel good about yourself. However, it is just a temporary fix and isn't a long-term solution. Money can buy you things, but it cannot buy happiness. Happiness comes from within, and it is an emotion. All the money in the world will not make you happy. It obviously does help ease your life, but that's about it. Focus on the things that matter to you.

Rejection Isn't Personal

We all face rejection at some point in our life. Don't take rejection personally, and think of it as an opportunity to learn. Think about the reasons that led to the rejection. Don't dwell on the fact that you didn't get something. Instead, take a minute and think about the reasons why you didn't get something. When you know the reasons, you can work to improve yourself. Rejection is part and parcel of life, and it helps you to grow and attain success.

Backup Plan

Prepare yourself for the worst-case scenario. You never know when the unexpected might happen. Whenever it does happen, it is better to have a plan instead of being caught unaware, isn't it? If you have a backup plan, it makes all the difference between success and failure at a critical point.

Social Skills Matter

You might like your alone time, but you cannot live your life like a recluse. Humans are social beings, and we all need social contact at some point of time or the other. Therefore, you need to work on your social skills as well. It doesn't mean that you need to spend all your time socializing but do it at times. Your social life can make you feel happy. It will help you concentrate on those people who matter to you.

Travel

If you want to develop your character, learn, and explore, then the best option is to travel. Get away from home and see new places. When you get away from the hustle and bustle of your daily life, you have an opportunity to appreciate all the good that you have in your life.

Don't Try to Multitask

Multitasking might make you feel like you can get a lot done at the same time. However, this isn't the case. When you try to multitask, you cannot fully concentrate on even a single task at hand. So, you effectively decrease your productivity and increase the time you spend on a task. Instead, work on one thing at a time before you move on to the next job.

Embrace Growth

Growth is essential in life. The precondition for growth is change. You need to embrace change if you want to grow. You need to develop a growth mindset that thrives on challenges. It will help you to face all the obstacles or challenges that occur during the course of your life.

Balance

You need to strike a balance between your personal and professional life. You must not give up on one to concentrate on the other. If you do this, you won't lead a fulfilling life. Your personal and professional lives are the two sides of the same coin. Learn to strike a balance between these two, and you will be happy.

Live in the Moment

Don't forget to live in the present. We all tend to plan so much for our future that we forget about the present altogether. If you ignore your present for a future that might or might not happen, you tend to give up a lot in your life. Plan for the future, but don't ignore the present.

Smile Often

Don't let small issues bog you down or make you feel blue. Not everything in life is to be taken seriously. Try looking at the positive side of any situation. You always have a choice: you can either feel hurt or you can let it go. Don't be pessimistic and learn to smile. A smile is contagious, and it helps to improve your overall mood.

Make it a point to smile as soon as you wake up. It will provide you with a positive mindset while starting a day. Remind yourself that you must often smile in a day. Set reminders or think about the things that make you smile. Create certain cues to smile. Make it a point to smile at everyone you make eye contact with. Smile often and the same will be reciprocated. Think happy thoughts and you will automatically start smiling. Try doing this, and you will see a positive change.

124

CONCLUSION

You have gone from gaining knowledge about the minimalist mindset to transitioning into it, with an eye toward decluttering as your first steps to be a minimalist. You are well on your way to a better life, with less clutter and more happiness.

There are still some steps you need to work on. Even though you have already begun your new habits, you have to face the setbacks and learn how to work through them.

You can go back to this book when you find an old habit return. You can reread the section that you might have suffered in and try again. You might need to go a little slower, you may need to speed up, or you might need to declutter a bit more than you have.

The journey is not easy. Emotions play a big role in what you are attempting. Do not lose hope. Find a support team and talk about your journey into the minimalist mindset as others have done.

The reward is what you decide, but one thing will always be true— you are going to be happier, less stressed, and have more time to do the things you love. Hard work is necessary. No one ever got anything in life for free that they didn't have to pay up for later. Eventually, the piper comes calling, whether for money to pay the debt gained or favor for all the favors received. Your hard work, sweat, tears, and pain will all be worth it when you are sipping margaritas on the next "National Margarita Day." Okay, maybe you will be sipping wine or enjoying a cruise because you have the time and savings. No matter what you gain—enjoy it!

Sources

https://www.theminimalists.com/radical/

https://www.apartmenttherapy.com/these-are-the-6-types-of-minimalists-which-one-are-you-250532

https://www.therusticelk.com/32-tips-on-becoming-a-minimalist/

https://www.apartmenttherapy.com/seeking-simplicity-how-to-start-living-a-more-minimal-lifestyle-210936

http://www.simplyfiercely.com/minimalism-goal-setting/

http://www.markmerrill.com/7-ways-to-know-whats-truly-important-to-you/

https://zenhabits.net/the-first-rule-of-simplifying-identify-the-essential-or-how-to-avoid-the-void/

https://clutterfreenow.com/blog/decluttering/decluttering-for-beginners-5-rules-to-encourage-you-to-let-go/

https://www.elitedaily.com/life/things-need-stop-immediately-want-live-stress-free-life/659777

http://www.beigerenegade.com/2016/02/25/seven-principles-for-decluttering-your-life/

Made in the USA
Middletown, DE
14 June 2019